Getting Started with Microsoft Viva

An End User Guide to Business Transformation

D'arce Hess
Albert-Jan Schot
Tracy van der Schyff

Getting Started with Microsoft Viva: An End User Guide to Business Transformation

D'arce Hess
Westford, Massachusetts, United States

Albert-Jan Schot
HENDRIK-IDO-AMBACHT, Zuid-Holland,
The Netherlands

Tracy van der Schyff
Centurion Gauteng, South Africa

ISBN-13 (pbk): 978-1-4842-8589-3
https://doi.org/10.1007/978-1-4842-8590-9

ISBN-13 (electronic): 978-1-4842-8590-9

Managing Director, Apress Media LLC: Welmoed Spahr
Acquisitions Editor: Joan Murray
Development Editor: Laura Berendson
Coordinating Editor: Jill Balzano

Cover photo by Josep Martins on Unsplash

Distributed to the book trade worldwide by Springer Science+Business Media LLC, 1 New York Plaza, Suite 4600, New York, NY 10004. Phone 1-800-SPRINGER, fax (201) 348-4505, e-mail orders-ny@springer-sbm.com, or visit www.springeronline.com. Apress Media, LLC is a California LLC and the sole member (owner) is Springer Science + Business Media Finance Inc (SSBM Finance Inc). SSBM Finance Inc is a **Delaware** corporation.

For information on translations, please e-mail booktranslations@springernature.com; for reprint, paperback, or audio rights, please e-mail bookpermissions@springernature.com.

Apress titles may be purchased in bulk for academic, corporate, or promotional use. eBook versions and licenses are also available for most titles. For more information, reference our Print and eBook Bulk Sales web page at http://www.apress.com/bulk-sales.

Any source code or other supplementary material referenced by the author in this book is available to readers on GitHub (https://github.com/Apress). For more detailed information, please visit http://www.apress.com/source-code.

Printed on acid-free paper

Table of Contents

About the Authors.. xiii

About the Technical Reviewer xv

Acknowledgments xvii

Part I: Microsoft Viva Introduction 1

Chapter 1: Introduction to Microsoft Viva 3

Reimagine the Employee Experience... 3

What Is Microsoft Viva?.. 4

Chapter 2: The Gears That Deliver Microsoft Viva 5

Overview of the Modules 6

Chapter 3: Features and Licensing 11

Microsoft Viva: Now and in the Future 11

Microsoft Viva Licensing 12

Part II: Microsoft Viva Learning..13

Chapter 4: Microsoft 365 Adoption..15

What Is Adoption? 15

The Impact of Training on Adoption.. 17

Different Training Methods Available 19

Learning Styles... 19

Learning Methods... 20

Changing Learning Cultures.. 22

Measurement and Analytics... 23

Microsoft 365 Usage Report.. 24

Microsoft 365 Usage Analytics 26

Microsoft Teams Analytics and Reporting 26

Microsoft Productivity Score 27

Chapter 5: Introduction to Microsoft Viva Learning 33

Product Overview.. 33

Why Use Microsoft Viva Learning?... 34

Chapter 6: Viva Learning for Administrators 37

Licensing.. 37

Standalone Subscriptions and Viva Suite 37

Free Viva Learning... 37

Free LinkedIn Learning Courses... 38

Roles 41

Adding the Knowledge Admin... 41

Set Up Microsoft Viva Learning 42

Pin the Viva Learning App for Employees 42

Block the Viva Learning App 43

Configure Your Learning Sources.. 44

SharePoint as a Content Source 45

Configure SharePoint as a Source for Viva Learning 46

Prepare the Source Material... 47

Reference the Source Material.. 49

Check the Access.. 50

Configure the Tracking of Recommended Content................................. 51

Create Featured Sets 52

Integration with Learning Management Systems 54

Using 3rd Party Content Providers 55

Chapter 7: Viva Learning for Employees and Managers **57**

  Navigation 57

    Pin the App in Teams 57

    Show Me Around 58

  Home Tab 59

    Engaging with Your Courses 61

    Pick Your Interests 61

  My Learning 62

    Navigation 62

    Courses Recommended to You 63

    Recommend Courses 64

    Sharing Courses 65

    Embed Learning into Chat Conversations 65

  Manage 67

    Manage Courses Recommended to Others 67

    Add Viva Learning as a Tab to Your Teams 68

  Closing 69

Part III: Microsoft Viva Connections **71**

Chapter 8: The Intranet **73**

  The Purpose of an Intranet 73

  The Intelligent Intranet 74

  The Challenge 74

Chapter 9: Introduction to Microsoft Viva Connections **75**

  Microsoft Viva Connections Overview 75

  Integration with Microsoft 365 Apps 76

  Core Concepts and Capabilities 77

    The Mobile Experience 78

    The Desktop Experience 79

    Curated vs. Tailored Experiences 80

    Language 80

Chapter 10: Preparation and Setup 81

    Intranet Groundwork 82

    Define the Home Site 83

        Using the SharePoint Admin Center 83

        Using PowerShell 84

    Navigate, Search, and Discover 84

        The Evolution of Finding Stuff 84

        Global Way Finding 86

    Configure Your Navigation 87

        The SharePoint App Bar and Global Navigation 88

    Create and Customize Your Dashboard 90

        Create Your Dashboard 91

        Adding Cards to Your Dashboard 92

        Configuring the Cards for Your Dashboard 93

        Planning the Layout of Your Dashboard 93

        Planning the Audience of Your Cards 94

        Access the Dashboard 95

    Plan and Create Content for Your Feed 97

    Configure the Viva Connections App in the Admin Center 97

    Set Up Policies for Desktop and Mobile Teams App 98

        Allow the Use of the App 99

    Change Management 100

    Closing 100

Part IV: Microsoft Viva Topics 101

Chapter 11: Introduction to Viva Topics 103

    Recommended Prerequisite Knowledge 104

        SharePoint 105

        Teams 105

        Yammer 107

        Current Licensing Requirements 110

        Summary 111

Chapter 12: Configuring Viva Topics.. 113

Technical Planning 113

Licensing 113

How to Apply Licenses.. 116

Configure Viva Topics 117

How Viva Topics Will Find Topics 118

Excluding Topics 122

Choose Who Can See Topics.. 124

Setting Viva Topics Permissions 127

Create a Topic Center 129

Summary.. 132

Chapter 13: Topics' Role in Knowledge Management...................... 133

What Is Knowledge Management? 133

Types of Knowledge.. 134

Where Does Viva Topics Fit In?.. 135

Common Search Issues that Viva Topics Can Help With 136

Conclusion 137

Chapter 14: Viva Topics' Roles and Responsibilities 139

Roles in Viva Topics.. 139

Administrators 139

Knowledge Manager.. 141

Topic Contributors 142

Summary.. 143

Chapter 15: Creating and Working with Topics and Topic Pages........ 145

AI-Suggested Topics 145

Types of AI-Suggested Topics... 146

Suggested Topics in Topic Center... 148

Confirm a Suggested Topic... 151

Published Topics... 152

Removed Topics.. 152

Manually Curated Topics 153

    Create a New Topic 153

    Remove a Topic Page 155

    Expected Time Frames 156

Understanding Security 156

    What Parts of a Topic Are Seen by Users 157

    What About Email or a User's OneDrive? 157

    Guests and External Users 157

Where Do Users See Topics 158

    SharePoint Highlights 158

    Search Results 159

    Office Application Search 160

    Yammer 160

    Microsoft Teams 162

    Topic Center 165

Language Support 165

    Summary 165

Part V: Microsoft Viva Insights **167**

Chapter 16: Employee Well-being **169**

Product Overview 169

Privacy 172

The Modules 173

    Personal Insights 173

    Manager Insights 174

    Leader Insights 175

    Analysis Capabilities 175

    Integration 175

Metrics 175

    Based on Your Work 176

    Questionnaires About Feelings 176

Stay in Control 177

    Block Time 177

    Praise People 177

    Briefing 177

Chapter 17: Licensing Viva Insights and Viva Insights Capacity 179

Insights by MyAnalytics 179

Viva Insights Add-On 180

Viva Insights Capacity Feature 181

Preparing Your Environment 181

Chapter 18: Personal Insights 183

Setup 183

    Microsoft Teams Setup 184

    Exchange Online Setup 185

Privacy 187

    Key Principles 188

Microsoft Teams App 188

    Reflect 190

    Send Praise 191

    Virtual Commute 193

    Headspace 194

    Stay Connected 194

    Protect Time 196

    Settings 196

Outlook Add-In 197

    Time Away 198

Dashboards 203

    Viva Insights Home 203

Email Reminders 208

    Briefing 208

    Digests 211

Conclusion 211

Chapter 19: Manager Insights **213**

Setup.. 213

Privacy 215

Team Insights... 215

    1:1 Reminders 216

    Quiet Hours Impact... 217

    Team Meeting Habits 217

Group Insights.. 218

Briefing and Digest E-Mails 218

    Digest E-Mail 219

Conclusion 219

Chapter 20: Leader Insights **221**

Setup.. 221

Privacy 221

Available Reports 222

    Organizational Resilience 222

    Employee Engagement.. 224

    Improve Agility.. 224

    Foster Innovation.. 224

    Effective Manager 225

    Operation Effectiveness.. 225

    Accelerate Change 225

    Transform Meeting Culture... 226

    Increase Customer Focus 226

Conclusion 226

Chapter 21: Advanced Insights.. **227**

Setup.. 227

Privacy 234

Plans 235

Analyze Data 237

Query Designer 237

Consumption Model 240

Peer Analysis 240

Conclusion 241

Appendix: Hyperlink Resources for the Book 243

Index 245

About the Authors

D'arce Hess is the Experience Design Lead for Digital Workplace at Takeda Pharmaceuticals. For more than 12 years, she has specialized in the creation of custom portals and experiences in SharePoint, Microsoft Teams, the Web, and Office365. As a UI/UX Designer and Developer, D'arce uses industry and Microsoft best practices as a base for creating solutions that simplify processes and drive user adoption and governance from the start. As a recognized Microsoft MVP, she has worked with Fortune 500 companies and has become a trusted partner to her clients in the industries of healthcare, pharmaceuticals, legal, travel and tourism, and entertainment. She loves to volunteer in the community and is the leader of the Rhode Island SharePoint User Group.

As a senior cloud architect, **Albert-Jan Schot** enjoys stepping up to the challenge of designing, developing, and building innovative cloud solutions. He is a valuable source of knowledge for his colleagues, customers, and the worldwide Microsoft community. With his no-nonsense and can-do mentality, he brings a unique combination of in-depth hands-on experience and consultancy skills on all levels to any team. As a CTO within BLIS.digital, Albert-Jan is responsible for the technical vision and strategy within the low-code practice.

Being rewarded as an MVP (Microsoft Most Valuable Professional) for both M365 Development and M365 Apps & Services, he is committed to helping others get the most out of their experience with Microsoft technologies, sharing his passion, real-world knowledge, and technical expertise with the community and with Microsoft.

ABOUT THE AUTHORS

 **Tracy van der Schyff** is a Microsoft 365 Coach and Catalyst, Blogger, YouTuber, Trainer, and Office Servers MVP. To facilitate the evolution of human capabilities, Tracy's passion is to empower people, and therefore training and change management lie close to her heart. Her mission is to positively impact WHAT and HOW people create, as she believes that what we design/create, designs/creates us back (Ontological Design). It is about enabling others to serve themselves better, expand their possibilities, increase their capacity to learn, act more effectively, and better design their future.

Endorsement

I met Tracy at SharePoint Saturday Johannesburg's speaker dinner, back in 2012.

She showed up wearing a crocheted beret and scarf, sitting at the corner of the table during dinner. I had no idea who she was, except that she was presenting at SharePoint Saturday that year. Fast forward ten years and she has become the definitive authority in Microsoft technology adoption, focusing on Microsoft 365.

I remember her presenting to customers in mid-2015 on all things computer literacy and how organizations can save money by just being able to find information effectively. At the same time, she translated her content management and information architecture skills into building world class intranets for some of South Africa's top commercial and public sector companies. Her unique approach to Enterprise Content Management and Content Services allows end users to untap the intrinsic value of the Microsoft technology landscape, with her starting with SharePoint initially and later extending her portfolio to include Microsoft Teams, Yammer, Planner, To Do, etc., as the products became generally available to customers across the globe. She has always remained unassuming and really has no idea of the impact of what she does.

Her personality and ethos shone through in everything that she did, especially when she got involved in driving community in South Africa with her approach to everything. Empowering people through her teachings, she embodies "learning through sharing" and the spirit of helping every single person she talks to.

As the world's most passionate Microsoft fan, she continues to change the world, one customer at a time, and I am fortunate enough to call her my dear friend. Find her online or at a conference, which she regularly keynotes, watch her content, read her ridiculous blogs on all things Microsoft 365. Your life will be better for it.

Alistair Pugin

CTO – NBConsult | Azure & Office MVP | Blogger | Podcaster | Speaker

About the Technical Reviewer

Treb Gatte, prior to becoming CEO of MarqueeInsights.com and TopLine.io, worked in leadership positions at Microsoft, Starbucks, and Wachovia (now Wells Fargo). He has been recognized as Data Platform MVP from Microsoft.

Treb lives in the Seattle area and holds an MBA from Wake Forest University.

Acknowledgments

There's a beautiful African word in the Bantu language – *Ubuntu.* It means "I am who I am, because of who we all are." A shout-out to my family and friends – who have always supported my crazy ideas and believed in me during the times when I didn't. My clients – who have taught me more than any course or certification ever could. And finally, the Microsoft Community – who gave my life meaning, a sense of belonging, and gave me a reason to get up for every single day.

I don't know everything, but I know everyone who does!

—Tracy

PART I

Microsoft Viva Introduction

Welcome to our introduction of Microsoft Viva. This book will not only share the technical "how to" for end users, managers, as well as administrators but will also focus on the most important aspect, why all of this is necessary. It tells a story of a world that needed change, the new modern workplace and resilience, and what led to the new digital employee experience (EX).

CHAPTER 1

Introduction to Microsoft Viva

Reimagine the Employee Experience

An awakening has taken place in a world where business results have always been the focus. Managers have realized that the greatest influence on the customer experience and eventually customer success have always been "under our noses." I am referring to our greatest assets, our employees. When putting your employees first, they put your customers first. But this new way of thinking has a much greater impact than just "your bottom line." When focusing on the well-being of our employees, we impact and change our work environments and company cultures, for the good.

One of my favorite quotes are *"If You Want Different Results, You Have to Try Different Approaches"* by Albert Einstein. In Microsoft's e-book *The People-Powered Workplace*, we are introduced to a new way of working, which requires new ways of thinking, a fresh perspective. As stated by Microsoft *"The challenge is to bring these capabilities together naturally, in the flow of everyday work, joined together in a way that empowers people and teams to be their best."* This forms the foundation and purpose of Microsoft Viva, and I believe it will change the way we work, forever. Below you'll see the elements identified as well as the modules aligned to these elements.

Apart from the 4 modules covered in this book (Topics, Connections, Learning & Insights), five new wellbeing and productivity modules are in the process of being made available: Amplify, Pulse, Sales and Goals. More detail on these can be found in the referenced repository.

© D'arce Hess, Albert-Jan Schot, Tracy van der Schyff 2023
D. Hess et al., *Getting Started with Microsoft Viva*, https://doi.org/10.1007/978-1-4842-8590-9_1

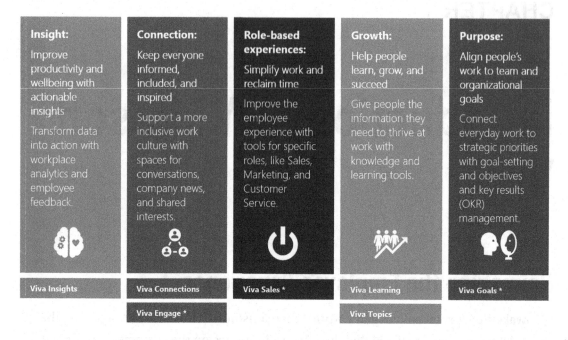

Figure 1-1. *A fresh perspective is needed: six elements*

> *An EXP is a digital platform that puts people at the center by bringing together systems of work with systems of support into an integrated employee experience. It provides people with the resources and support they need to succeed and thrive, no matter their location.*

> —Microsoft

What Is Microsoft Viva?

The Microsoft Viva Family will deliver the integrated employee experience platform (EXP) that empowers employees to thrive in the new digital era within Microsoft 365. This platform will ensure that people stay connected and are supported within their Microsoft Teams ecosystem.

> *Microsoft Viva, the first employee experience platform to bring tools for employee engagement, learning, wellbeing, and knowledge discovery, directly into the flow of people's work. Viva is designed to help employees learn, grow, and thrive, with new experiences that integrate with the productivity and collaboration capabilities in Microsoft 365 and Microsoft Teams.*

> —Microsoft

CHAPTER 2

The Gears That Deliver Microsoft Viva

To create the holistic employee experience and support the elements that do so (Connections, Insights, Purpose, Growth and Role-based experiences), 8 modules will be utilized:

1. Viva Connections

2. Viva Engage

3. Viva Insights

4. Viva Learning

5. Viva Topics

6. Viva Sales

7. Viva Pulse

8. Viva Amplify

In this book we will cover Connections, Insights, Learning & Topics. More details on Sales, Engage as well as the new Pulse & Amplify can be found in the referenced repository.

© D'arce Hess, Albert-Jan Schot, Tracy van der Schyff 2023
D. Hess et al., *Getting Started with Microsoft Viva*, https://doi.org/10.1007/978-1-4842-8590-9_2

Viva Connections:
Keep everyone informed, connected, and inspired to bring their best to work every day.

Viva Learning:
Empower people to gain targeted skills in the apps they already use, so everyone can learn and grow.

Viva Topics:
Free up time by making it easy for people to find information and put knowledge to work.

Viva Insights:
Give leaders, managers, and employees data-driven, privacy-protected insights that help everyone work smarter and thrive.

We need to maintain culture, connect employees, and harness human ingenuity in a hybrid world.

Jared Spataro
Corporate Vice President
Microsoft

Figure 2-1. *Microsoft Viva the Employee Experience Platform (EXP)*

Overview of the Modules

As illustrated, Microsoft Viva currently consists of four modules designed to deliver the new employee experience. See Figures 2-2 to 2-5 for a glimpse before we get started on our journey of exploring these products.

> **Viva Learning:** Empower people to gain targeted skills in the apps they already use, so everyone can learn and grow.

> **Viva Connections:** Keep everyone informed, connected, and inspired to bring their best to work every day.

> **Viva Topics:** Free up time by making it easy for people to find information and put knowledge to work.

> **Viva Insights:** Give leaders, managers, and employees data-driven, privacy-protected insights that help everyone work smarter and thrive.

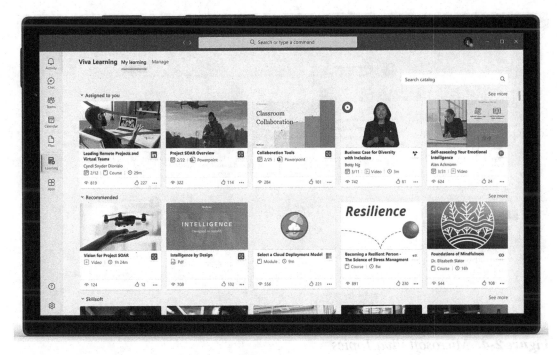

Figure 2-2. *Microsoft Viva Learning*

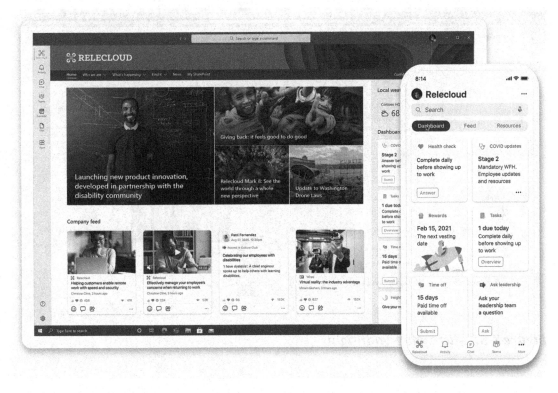

Figure 2-3. *Microsoft Viva Connections*

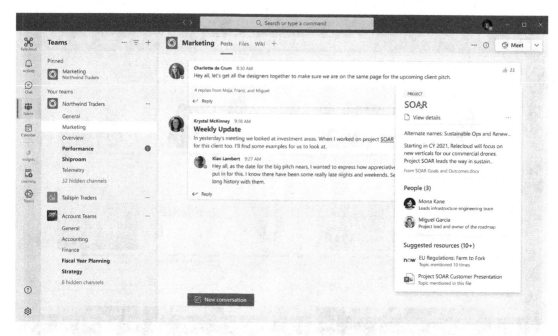

Figure 2-4. *Microsoft Viva Topics*

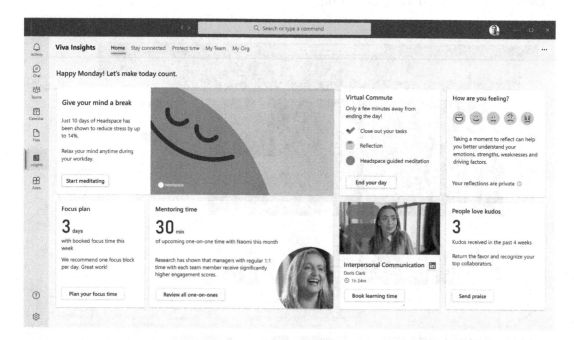

Figure 2-5. *Microsoft Viva Insights*

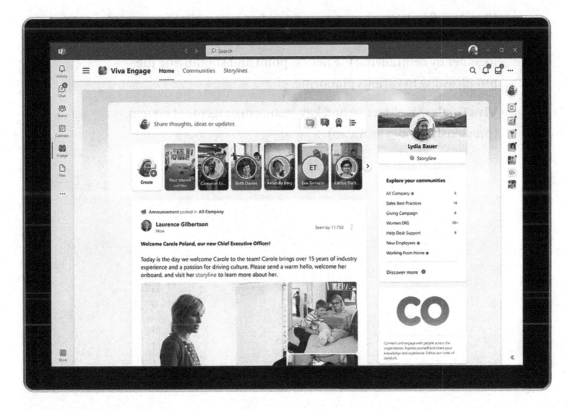

Figure 2-6. *Viva Engage*

For a glimpse into what you can expect from the additional modules, see below:

Viva Sales: Designed to help employees work seamlessly between Microsoft 365, Microsoft Teams and their CRM for a greater selling experience and simplified data capturing related to customer engagements.

Viva Engage: This module is the evolution of the current Yammer Communities App available in Microsoft 365. New features have been added to support the strengthening of relationships and knowledge sharing.

Viva Pulse: Created to empower leaders in gathering feedback from their teams.

Viva Amplify: With so many apps and features available for communications within Microsoft 365, Amplify brings it all together by centralizing the access point and simplifying the broadcasting to various platforms.

Viva Goals: An objective and key results management system (previously known as Aly.io)

CHAPTER 3

Features and Licensing

Microsoft Viva: Now and in the Future

Although this book gives an overview of the 4 original modules, Microsoft announced the acquisition of Ally.io (now known as Viva Goals) on October 7, 2021. Personally, I am excited about this, as I have always said that if a job profile, task, project, and/or initiative does not support and help realize the company's strategic objectives, there simply is no meaning and motivation for it.

Viva Goals could help to fill this gap in the Viva Family as its purpose is to align the company's strategic objectives and core priorities with the work the employee already focuses on. And as it will form part of the Viva Modules, it will also empower employees, through its integration with the existing employee experience platform (EXP).

Viva Sales, Amplify and Pulse was announced on the 22 of September 2022.

Viva Learning:
Empower people to gain targeted skills in the apps they already use, so everyone can learn and grow.

Viva Connections:
Keep everyone informed, connected, and inspired to bring their best to work every day.

Viva Topics:
Free up time by making it easy for people to find information and put knowledge to work.

Viva Insights:
Give leaders, managers, and employees data-driven, privacy-protected insights that help everyone work smarter and thrive.

Figure 3-1. *Microsoft Viva Extended Family*

© D'arce Hess, Albert-Jan Schot, Tracy van der Schyff 2023
D. Hess et al., *Getting Started with Microsoft Viva*, https://doi.org/10.1007/978-1-4842-8590-9_3

Microsoft Viva Licensing

For up to date information regarding licensing options, costs and features included in different plans, refer to "Microsoft Viva Plans and Pricing" as well as the comparison table made available for download. `https://www.microsoft.com/en-za/microsoft-viva/pricing`.

PART II

Microsoft Viva Learning

Microsoft Viva Learning is the Center for Learning of Microsoft 365 within Microsoft Teams. Here employees can discover training content, learn, share, and recommend training to others. Content can be surfaced from LinkedIn Learning, Microsoft Learn, Microsoft 365 Training and other third-party learning content providers.

CHAPTER 4

Microsoft 365 Adoption

I know you're excited to start edufcating yourself about Viva Learning. But before we can get started, I need to share some concepts and principles with you on adoption, learning cultures and measurements. Although your Viva Learning will be used for more than courses related to technology, the psychology behind learning stays the same. These same principles can be applied to the introduction of Microsoft Viva in your company. After all, we are only human and to resist change comes naturally.

—Tracy

What Is Adoption?

In recent years, adoption has become a popular topic of discussion, and although well researched and documented, still very misunderstood and often not approached right. Perhaps it is all about perspectives and that IT and Business often interpret it different due to unique needs and requirements.

Now of course, what we are referring to is the act of introducing a new technology/platform to a company, and then ensuring that the employees are aware of the changes and "can" use it. Traditionally companies would embark on a Change Management Journey. And regardless of the methodology or framework they use, the focus would always be on Communication and Training (in my eyes, it is all about communication, as I believe training to be a form of communication).

Out of this IT/Business disparity, another confusion was born. And that is that consumption seems to be a measurement of or the equivalent of adoption. To fully understand adoption, let us first clarify "Consumption" and "Adoption."

Consumption. This would be the number of people using specific products (activities/usage) during a particular period.

D. Hess et al., *Getting Started with Microsoft Viva*, https://doi.org/10.1007/978-1-4842-8590-9_4

Adoption. This is the acceptance and integration of said technology, but more importantly, being empowered to be efficient at using it.

Figure 4-1 gives an overview of how this translates in our personal lives.

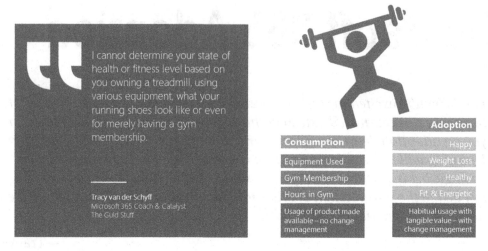

Figure 4-1. Consumption vs. Adoption

Perhaps now we can agree that although consumption or usage delivers a specific measurement for adoption, it does not represent adoption in totality. To achieve true adoption, we need to invest resources to change company cultures, and importantly, the behavior and mindset of our greatest assets, our employees. If you are new to change management, the "*Microsoft Service Adoption Specialist Course*" is a must and will give you the necessary knowledge and tools to not only understand the task at hand, but also enable you to be instrumental in driving organizational and behavioral change in your company.

In the *Accelerating Modern Workplace Productivity Adoption* e-book, Microsoft identified four phases in the journey to adopting *new ways of working*.

- Deployment: This is the process of implementing/deploying the technical Microsoft 365 infrastructure and the assigning of licenses and apps to the employees.

- Usage: This refers to employees using the technology made available to them. For example: they no longer have file shares and now use OneDrive.

- Adoption: During this phase, employees start changing their habits and using the new technology becomes ingrained in their daily routine.

- Proficiency: Through adoption, employees become more efficient which enables overall proficiency for their team, department, and eventually the company. This is where digital transformation is triggered.

As adoption requires more than traditional change management, the resources Microsoft has made available on their Microsoft 365 Adoption Hub are invaluable. The journeys are defined by roles as well as products and supply all the digital resources you could ever need. All these activities fit neatly into the adoption framework as illustrated in Figure 4-2.

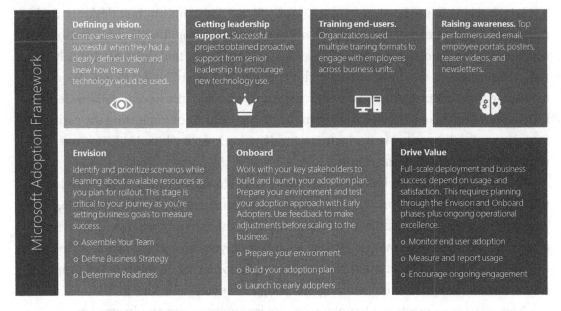

Figure 4-2. *Microsoft Adoption Framework*

The Impact of Training on Adoption

If I had a dollar for each time someone said, "*Users are so difficult, they resist change,*" I would be sitting in The Bahamas, sipping cocktails. It is rather easy to blame resistance on the character of a person or even their age, but after years of research and painful experience, I have learnt that it is much more complicated than that. It is all about our comfort zones, and our fear of technology. Yes, I said "fear," and perhaps you have not realized yet that your employees have an unconscious fear of the technology they have had to use for years. With that said, I do believe that there are two main reasons behind this fear.

- The IT support process
- Lack of efficient training

Let us first talk about the **IT support process**. In the past, we locked down as much as we could and only gave our employees enough information to keep them out of trouble. When they logged calls, we would fix their issues for them, not showing them how to troubleshoot it for themselves, or even what caused it. Now of course we did some of this to protect our environments, or due to availability of resources, but it did have a serious impact on the self-esteem of our employees.

It is shocking to see how many employees still use shortcuts on their desktops and navigate to files instead of using Search, not even knowing that the Windows Button searches for files, programs, and settings. As a trainer, I know that the most difficult part of training is to remember to teach those things I have already forgotten. We tend to assume that others already know what we know, and then the necessary knowledge transfer does not take place. This led to many of our employees not having the essential foundational skills needed to navigate the modern workplace which leads into my next reason, **the lack of efficient training**.

We only know what we know, to ask employees to let us know when they need training would then not work. Especially not in an environment like Microsoft 365, where thousands of new features have been added to help them be more efficient and effective. Also due to the low self-esteem, many employees are too embarrassed to raise their hand and ask for help. Another contributing factor is that our employees simply do not have time to sit in training, although training does eventually save them time.

Now apart from creating a happier work environment where employees are empowered to use the available technology, are not struggling, and are not frustrated, training will also save time, and thus, save money. In research done for Microsoft by Forrester "The Total Economic Impact™ Of Microsoft Teams," it was estimated that "*4 Hours per week are saved by information workers through improved collaboration and information sharing.*" Without doing any serious calculations, that is 10% of your salary bill. Read that again.

Today, every employee should be an empowered digital citizen. The greatest benefit of training users to use the various Microsoft 365 apps and services is that it supports the development of their digital literacy skills, as seen in (meant to be illustrative, but not exhaustive) Figure 4-3.

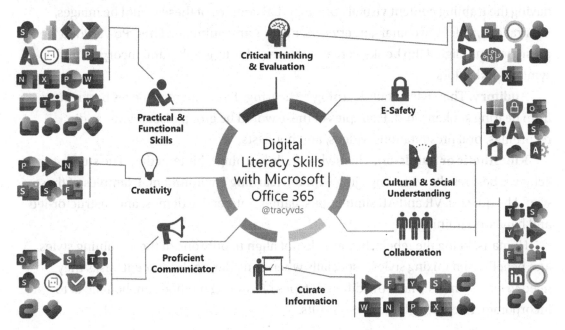

Figure 4-3. *Office 365 supports the development of digital literacy skills*

Different Training Methods Available

Over the years, we have seen many different training methods designed, documented, and made available for training programs. Before we look at the training methods available, I will first discuss the basic learning styles.

Learning Styles

- Reading/Writing
- Visual
- Auditory
- Kinesthetic

Reading/Writing. This style entails learning by reading and writing (taking of notes). The student achieves best results by reading the training content. Examples of these would be books, articles, blogs, checklists, training guides, and manuals.

Visual. This style entails learning by seeing. The student achieves best results from having the training content visually presented. Examples of these would be images, illustrations, videos, webinars, interviews, memes and animated GIFs, PowerPoint presentations, digital flip books, screen captures, charts, graphs, and incorporating symbols and colors.

Auditory. This style entails learning by hearing. The student achieves best results from hearing spoken word. Examples of these would be group discussions, audio recordings, oral presentations, videos, and podcasts.

Kinesthetic or hands-on. This style entails learning by interacting. The student achieves best results when engaging with the learning environment. Examples of these would be quizzes, VR and AR simulations, games, interactive demos, and instructor-led and hands-on training.

Humans, being the rebels they are, do not align to only one of these training styles and benefit from mixing styles, especially when considering the content/tasks they need to learn. This is where the different types of training methods are beneficial to incorporate different styles for best results.

Learning Methods

- Instructor-led training

  - This refers to training facilitated by an instructor. Traditionally, this would have been in person, but now also allows for online engagements. Examples could be: Webinars, Workshops, Lectures, One-on-one, and Classrooms with smaller groups of learners.

- eLearning

  - eLearning of course refers to the use of technology to deliver the training. Also known as online or electronic training delivery.

- Simulation training

  - Simulation training requires the creation of a learning environment that mirrors real-life working scenarios.

- Hands-on training

  - By far the most effective learning method allows for the employee to learn while performing the task under the supervision of the trainer/facilitator.

- Coaching or mentoring

  - These methods tend to focus less on technical skills and more on business and personal soft skills. The focus would be on listening, feedback loops, and celebrating successes.

- Lectures and group discussions

  - Allowing for more discussions, these learning methods invite feedback and debates to broaden the student's understanding of the topic.

- Role-playing

  - Also known as experimental learning, this method requires participants to act out different roles and interact in a scripted manner.

- Case studies

  - Case studies are all about "problem solving." Similar to group discussions, a case study will be given as pre-work to then discuss and find solutions.

Figure 4-4 gives an overview of the styles and methods available that should be incorporated in your training programs and approaches.

Figure 4-4. *Training style and methods*

Keep in mind that employees who have grown accustomed to printed training manuals over the years, would struggle to adopt to video training only, without the necessary change management.

Over the next few chapters, you will gain a better understanding of the impact of training and how to incorporate these different styles/methods into your employees' daily working lives.

Changing Learning Cultures

The saying *"you can lead a horse to water, but you can't make him drink"* applies so much to training, it could have been written specifically for it. In my nearly 20 years working with SharePoint and later Microsoft | Office 365, this was proven to me time and time again. What am I referring to, you might ask? Well, it insinuates that most people will not learn on their own, even when content is made available. I am NOT saying that people do not want to empower themselves, the sad truth is that most companies' culture and strategic objectives are not supportive of this.

Microsoft's corporate mission is *"to empower every person and every organization on the planet to achieve more."* This statement is not only focused externally, but also embraced internally by encouraging employees to allocate time to learning and evolving. Time being the magic word here and as we are finding ourselves in a time where autonomy fosters innovation, the knowledge to do so is crucial. Microsoft's commitment toward changing their company culture for the better is obvious from their "refreshed" leadership principles (Figure 4-5).

It is therefore imperative that companies not only invest in the technology to support learning cultures in their companies, but also engage in campaigns to change the learning cultures of employees AND ensure that job descriptions and KPI's represent and allow the time for employees to do so.

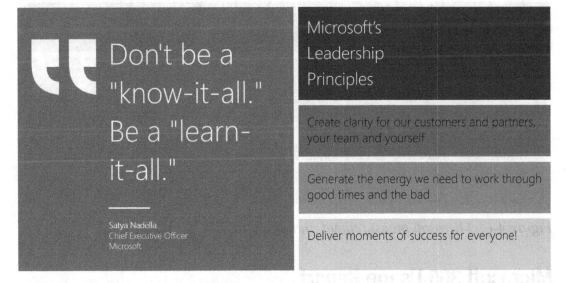

Figure 4-5. *Microsoft's leadership principles*

Measurement and Analytics

Measurement is an important part of the adoption process where we should track both usage and behavior. Without having detail of previous and future states, you will never be able to say whether the transition was successful or not. Especially when deploying learning platforms, the ability to track behavioral change plays an instrumental role in your company's digital transformation.

Microsoft supplies us with various reports and analytics to help us analyze the progress, and then implement corrective actions for greater/different results.

As you might be reading this, without having the necessary administration rights on your company's tenant, I will share the information and some screenshots to give you an oversight (Figure 4-6).

- Microsoft 365 Usage Report

- Microsoft 365 Usage Analytics (Power BI)

- Microsoft Teams Analytics and Reporting

- Microsoft Productivity Score

- User Satisfaction Surveys

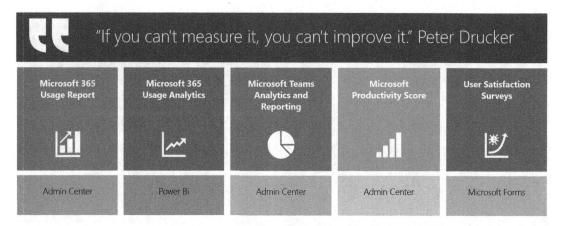

Figure 4-6. *Microsoft measurement and analytics*

Microsoft 365 Usage Report

The Microsoft 365 Usage Report is a great tool to use when identifying who uses which services a lot and whether quotas are reached. Figures 4-7 and 4-8 will show the activities tracked.

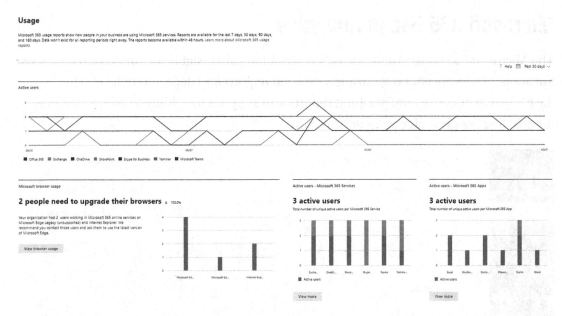

Figure 4-7. *Microsoft 365 usage report first section*

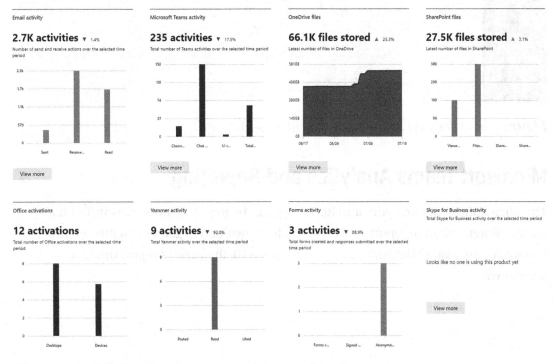

Figure 4-8. *Microsoft 365 usage report second section*

Microsoft 365 Usage Analytics

The Microsoft 365 Usage Analytics uses Power BI to gain insights on how various services are adopted withing your organization down to regions and department level. The dashboard includes several pre-built reports and supplies the ability to create custom reports. See Figure 4-9 for more information.

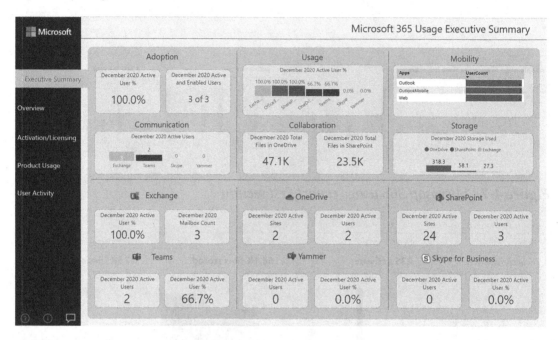

Figure 4-9. *Microsoft 365 usage – executive summary*

Microsoft Teams Analytics and Reporting

The Microsoft Teams Analytics and Reporting can be found in the Microsoft Teams admin center. Different reports are available for download to gather insights on how employees are using Microsoft Teams. In Figure 4-10, the various report options are shown:

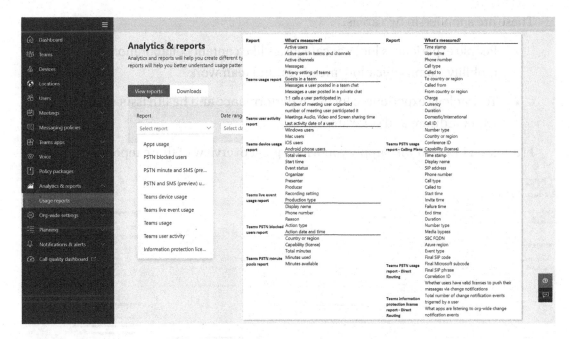

Figure 4-10. *Microsoft Teams Analytics – available reports*

Microsoft Productivity Score

The Microsoft Productivity Score can be found in the Microsoft 365 admin center under reports. Of all the reports available, I find this report most valuable as it tracks behavior and not just consumption (usage).

For more information on the Productivity Score and how it gets calculated, see the Microsoft Productivity Score documentation.

The report provides the following:

- Metrics supplies the actual data which can be used to determine your company's progress in their digital transformation journey.

- Insights about the data deliver the analytics on the preceding metrics to help with making decisions and identifying opportunities for improvement.

- Recommended actions are guidelines and resources from Microsoft to facilitate the change in behaviors.

These are supplied in two areas:

- People experiences looks at categories like content collaboration, mobility, communication, meetings, and teamwork.

- Technology experiences focus on performance and health issues with your hardware and software.

Figures 4-11 to 4-15 will supply you with a great overview of these reports.

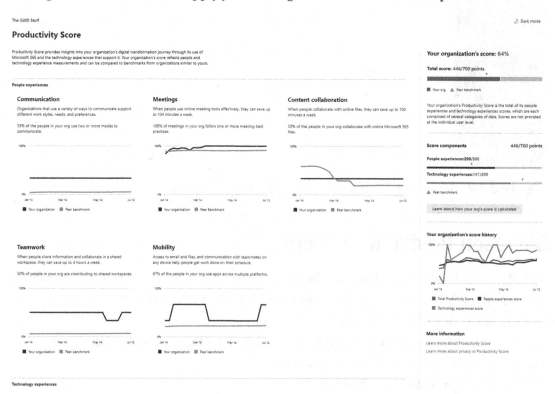

Figure 4-11. *Microsoft Productivity Score – main dashboard*

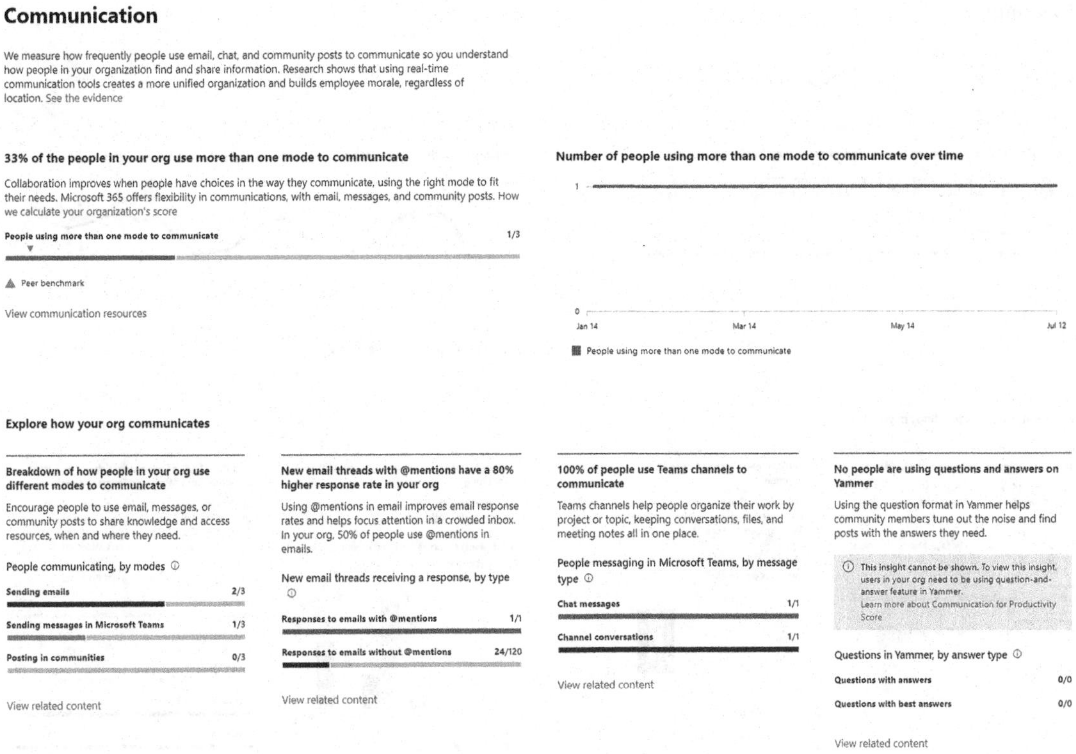

Communication

We measure how frequently people use email, chat, and community posts to communicate so you understand how people in your organization find and share information. Research shows that using real-time communication tools creates a more unified organization and builds employee morale, regardless of location. See the evidence

33% of the people in your org use more than one mode to communicate

Collaboration improves when people have choices in the way they communicate, using the right mode to fit their needs. Microsoft 365 offers flexibility in communications, with email, messages, and community posts. How we calculate your organization's score

People using more than one mode to communicate   1/3
▼

▲ Peer benchmark

View communication resources

Number of people using more than one mode to communicate over time

1 ───

0 ├─────────────┬─────────────────┬─────────────────┬──────────────
  Jan 14   Mar 14   May 14   Jul 12

■ People using more than one mode to communicate

Explore how your org communicates

Breakdown of how people in your org use different modes to communicate

Encourage people to use email, messages, or community posts to share knowledge and access resources, when and where they need.

People communicating, by modes ⓘ

Sending emails	2/3
Sending messages in Microsoft Teams	1/3
Posting in communities	0/3

View related content

New email threads with @mentions have a 80% higher response rate in your org

Using @mentions in email improves email response rates and helps focus attention in a crowded inbox. In your org, 50% of people use @mentions in emails.

New email threads receiving a response, by type ⓘ

Responses to emails with @mentions	1/1
Responses to emails without @mentions	24/120

View related content

100% of people use Teams channels to communicate

Teams channels help people organize their work by project or topic, keeping conversations, files, and meeting notes all in one place.

People messaging in Microsoft Teams, by message type ⓘ

Chat messages	1/1
Channel conversations	1/1

View related content

No people are using questions and answers on Yammer

Using the question format in Yammer helps community members tune out the noise and find posts with the answers they need.

ⓘ This insight cannot be shown. To view this insight, users in your org need to be using question-and-answer feature in Yammer. Learn more about Communication for Productivity Score

Questions in Yammer, by answer type ⓘ

Questions with answers	0/0
Questions with best answers	0/0

View related content

Figure 4-12. *Microsoft Productivity Score – communication*

Meetings

Research shows that when people use online meeting tools effectively, they improve the quality of their meetings and can save up to 104 minutes per week. To determine your Meetings score, we measure the use of meeting best practices, including using video, screen-sharing, and app and file-sharing. We're continually adding best practices to this report. See the evidence

100% of meetings in your org include one or more meeting best practices

Meetings where people understand the goal, are able to attend no matter where they are, and have clear next steps help build an inclusive culture and more efficient decision-making. How we calculate your organization's score

▲ Peer benchmark

View resources about meetings

Number of meetings organized and conducted with best practices over time

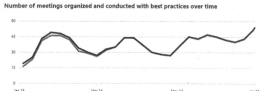

■ Meetings with best practices ■ All Meetings

Explore more about meetings in your org

94% of meetings had someone with video on	100% of people spend over 10 hours a week in meetings	Less than 1% of instant meetings are less than 30 minutes long	Less than 1%% of people participate in instant meetings from Microsoft Teams channels

Turning on the video during meetings makes people feel more included and the sessions more engaging.

Meetings with best practices in Microsoft Teams, by type ⓘ

| Video | 51/54 |
| Screensharing | 45/54 |

View related actions

Help ensure that people make good use of the time they spend in meetings with tools that help them feel engaged and productive.

Meeting attendees, broken out by total hours in meetings per week ⓘ

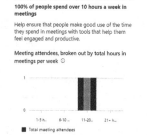

■ Total meeting attendees
■ Attendees in meetings with video
■ Attendees in meetings with screen-sharing

Instant meetings can help people quickly resolve issues and make decisions.

Percent of instant and scheduled meetings, broken out by meeting length ⓘ

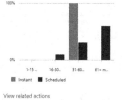

■ Instant ■ Scheduled

View related actions

Holding instant meetings from a Microsoft Teams channel creates transparency and helps with decision making. Encourage people to record these sessions to help keep coworkers informed.

Meeting attendees, across meeting types ⓘ

Instant 1:1 calls	1/1
Instant group calls	0/1
Instant Meet now in channel	0/1
Scheduled one-off meetings	1/1
Scheduled recurring meetings	1/1

View related actions

Figure 4-13. *Microsoft Productivity Score – meetings*

Content collaboration

We measure the number of people who create, read, and collaborate (edit and share) online for this part of your score. When people collaborate with online files, each person saves an average of 100 minutes, or almost 2 hours, per week. See the evidence

33% of people in your org collaborate with online Office files

When people create and read files online, they are more likely to collaborate online as well. We define content collaboration as one person creating and sharing an Office file, and then at least one other person reading it. This data contributes to your overall productivity score. How we calculate your organization's score

Readers	2/3
Creators	2/3
Collaborators	1/3

▲ Peer benchmark

View content collaboration resources

Number of readers, creators, and collaborators over time

■ Readers ■ Creators ■ Collaborators

Explore how your org collaborates

100% of people who use Office create files in OneDrive or SharePoint

Creating files in OneDrive or SharePoint means they're backed up, available from other devices, and set up for real-time collaboration.

People creating files, by location ⓘ

| OneDrive | 2/2 |
| SharePoint | 1/2 |

View related content

100% of people share files as an email attachment

Sharing a link to a file in the cloud instead of attaching a copy in email makes sharing more secure and allows users to collaborate in real time.

People sharing files in email, by type ⓘ

| Attach physical files | 2/2 |
| Link to online files | 0/2 |

View related content

33% of people share content externally

Customize SharePoint's external sharing settings to help people collaborate with external partners or people in your organization who have different licenses.

People sharing content ⓘ

| Share externally | 1/3 |
| Only share internally | 0/3 |

View related content

33% of people collaborate on 4 or more Office files

Invite people to learn about saving and sharing files in the cloud, co-authoring in real time, and collaborating with @mentions.

People collaborating, by number of shared files ⓘ

11 or more files	1/3
4-10 files	0/3
1-3 files	0/3
No collaboration	2/3

Figure 4-14. *Microsoft Productivity Score – content collaboration*

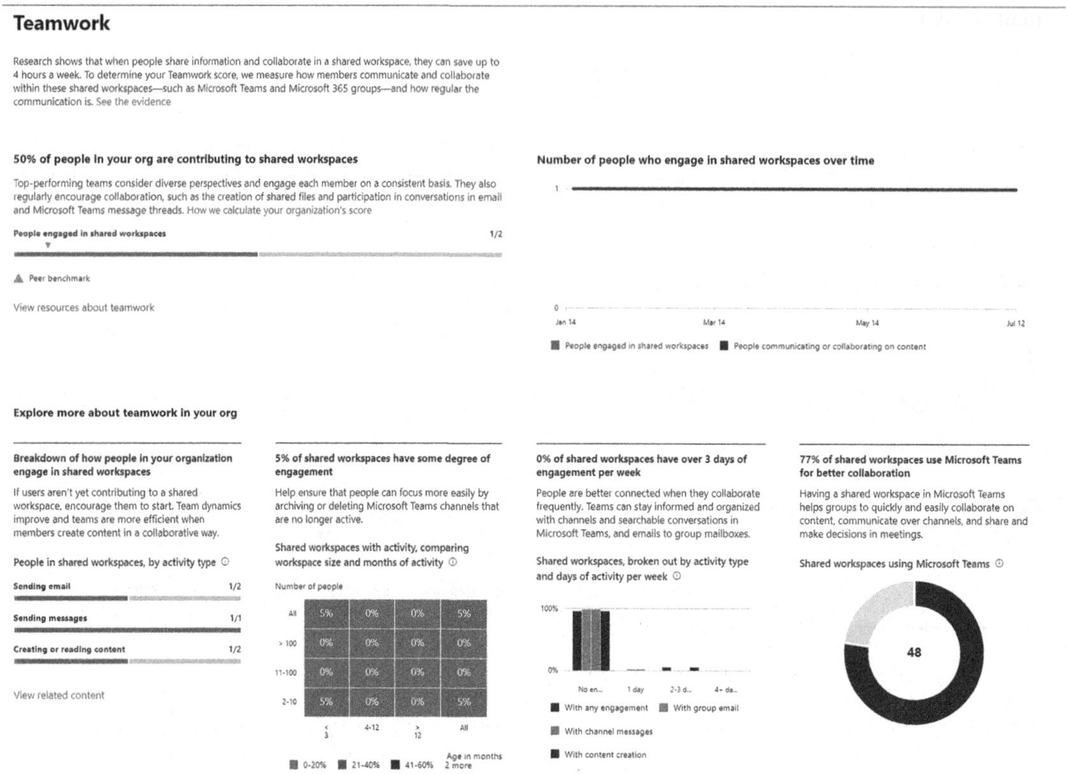
Teamwork
Research shows that when people share information and collaborate in a shared workspace, they can save up to 4 hours a week. To determine your Teamwork score, we measure how members communicate and collaborate within these shared workspaces—such as Microsoft Teams and Microsoft 365 groups—and how regular the communication is. See the evidence
50% of people in your org are contributing to shared workspaces
Top-performing teams consider diverse perspectives and engage each member on a consistent basis. They also regularly encourage collaboration, such as the creation of shared files and participation in conversations in email and Microsoft Teams message threads. How we calculate your organization's score
People engaged in shared workspaces
1/2
Peer benchmark
View resources about teamwork
Number of people who engage in shared workspaces over time
People engaged in shared workspaces
People communicating or collaborating on content
Explore more about teamwork in your org
Breakdown of how people in your organization engage in shared workspaces
If users aren't yet contributing to a shared workspace, encourage them to start. Team dynamics improve and teams are more efficient when members create content in a collaborative way.
People in shared workspaces, by activity type
Sending email 1/2
Sending messages 1/1
Creating or reading content 1/2
View related content
5% of shared workspaces have some degree of engagement
Help ensure that people can focus more easily by archiving or deleting Microsoft Teams channels that are no longer active.
Shared workspaces with activity, comparing workspace size and months of activity
Number of people
Age in months
0% of shared workspaces have over 3 days of engagement per week
People are better connected when they collaborate frequently. Teams can stay informed and organized with channels and searchable conversations in Microsoft Teams, and emails to group mailboxes.
Shared workspaces, broken out by activity type and days of activity per week
With any engagement
With group email
With channel messages
With content creation
77% of shared workspaces use Microsoft Teams for better collaboration
Having a shared workspace in Microsoft Teams helps groups to quickly and easily collaborate on content, communicate over channels, and share and make decisions in meetings.
Shared workspaces using Microsoft Teams
48

***Figure 4-15.** Microsoft Productivity Score - teamwork*

CHAPTER 5

Introduction to Microsoft Viva Learning

Product Overview

With the launch of Microsoft Viva, Microsoft published an e-book, *The People-Powered Workplace*. As a trainer and change management specialist, I loved seeing the focus placed on learning, as seen by the quotes from this e-book in Figure 5-1.

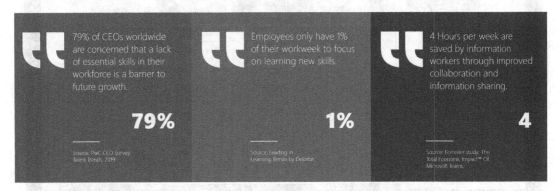

Figure 5-1. *The People-Powered Workplace*

Microsoft Viva Learning is the Center for Learning of Microsoft 365 in Microsoft Teams. Here employees can discover training content, learn, share, and recommend training to others. In the Home view inside of Microsoft Teams, content can be surfaced from LinkedIn Learning, Microsoft Learn, Microsoft 365 Training as well as 3rd party providers (based on existing subscriptions).

For a customizable learning experience, internal content can be surfaced from SharePoint based on permissions or job profiles, a great value-add for company-specific training, for example, induction programs, health and safety, and cross-training.

© D'arce Hess, Albert-Jan Schot, Tracy van der Schyff 2023
D. Hess et al., *Getting Started with Microsoft Viva*, https://doi.org/10.1007/978-1-4842-8590-9_5

Learning will surface across the other Viva modules, sure to enhance your learning experience, **Viva Insights** will help you set aside time for learning, **Viva Topics** will show learning suggestions and other knowledge resources, and in the **Viva Connections** app, you will find learning content in the company dashboard.

As mentioned, content can be recommended to individuals and groups. As a manager or team lead, you can see courses you have recommended and check the completion status on these. As the purpose of Viva Learning is to bring together learning content in one place (Microsoft Teams) and support learning as a natural part of your employees' day, it does not fulfill the traditional Learning Management System functions. This can be achieved by integrating your existing Learning Management System. As seen in Figure 5-2, Viva Learning blends seamlessly with Microsoft Teams.

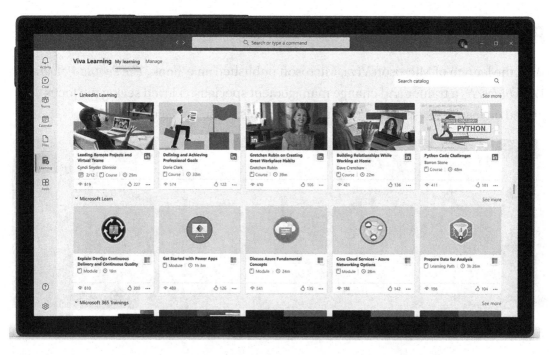

Figure 5-2. *Microsoft Viva Learning embedded in Microsoft Teams*

Why Use Microsoft Viva Learning?

Traditionally, training took us away from our workplace or desk. This resulted in many employees not participating in training, as they simply could not "take the day off." Training also took place with much bigger intervals, often once a year (linked to company budget). Now, more than ever, with so many employees working from home, the need to incorporate learning into our daily lives have become a necessity.

The concept of autonomy in the technology we use also drives a desire to take charge of our own digital destiny, so to speak. The ability to do so, as part of our workday, in the place where we are already working is what Viva Learning is all about.

To rest my brain and gain productivity, I often interchange "working tasks" with "learning tasks" or "creative tasks." Think of the Pomodoro Technique or the Ultradian Rhythm, but with a difference. Now, with Viva Learning, you will be able to build bite-sizes of learning into your day and continue to invest in your greatest asset – **you**.

In Figure 5-3, I have highlighted some benefits and, over the next couple of chapters, you will see even more benefits as I discuss the features available for each role player: administrator, manager, and employee.

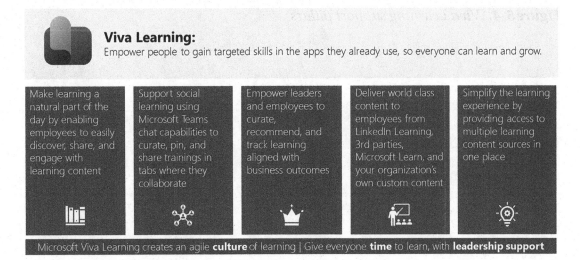

Figure 5-3. *Microsoft Viva Learning benefits*

Viva Learning puts your employees at the center by allowing learning while working, simplifying the process, and making it personal and relevant. Figure 5-4 illustrates the platform that allows Microsoft to deliver this.

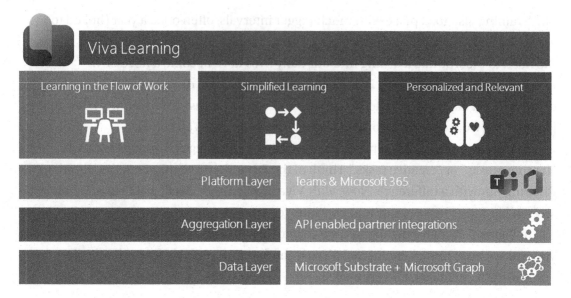

Figure 5-4. *Viva Learning support pillars*

CHAPTER 6

Viva Learning for Administrators

Licensing

Standalone Subscriptions and Viva Suite

The base license for Viva Learning is included in the following Microsoft 365 / Office 365 Plans: F1; F3; E1; E3; Business & E5. Additional features can be unlocked by purchasing the standalone Viva Learning Subscription, or the Viva Suite & Viva Suite Glint (minimum 100 users) Subscription. For more up to date information regarding licensing, refer to the Microsoft Viva plans and pricing resource.

Free Viva Learning

You might have noticed that you have Viva Learning as an app, to be added in Microsoft Teams, without having a separate subscription. This is due to Microsoft making a subset of capabilities available for free.

This free version will give you access to LinkedIn Learning, Microsoft Learn, Microsoft 365 Training and your own SharePoint content. No 3rd party providers can be added, and you will not be able to recommend content, or have access to the more advanced admin features. In Table 6-1, I've highlighted the features available as part of your Microsoft/Office 365 Microsoft Teams subscription and the additional features from the Viva Learning Subscription:

© D'arce Hess, Albert-Jan Schot, Tracy van der Schyff 2023
D. Hess et al., *Getting Started with Microsoft Viva*, https://doi.org/10.1007/978-1-4842-8590-9_6

Table 6-1. *Viva Learning feature comparison*

Included in your Microsoft Teams Subscription	Additional with your Viva Learning or Suite Subscriptions
Access Viva Learning in Microsoft Teams	Recommend content and track reported completion progress
Access to 125 free LinkedIn Learning courses, as well as the full library of Microsoft Learn and Microsoft 365 Trainings.	Integration with partner content providers
Integration of the full LinkedIn Learning library (separate subscription required).	Integration with learning management systems
Search, share, and chat about learning content	Add learning content to calendar with suggested time slots
Create learning tabs in Teams channels	Surface learning content in Microsoft Search across Bing.com, Office.com, and SharePoint.com
Organization-generated learning content with SharePoint and Viva Learning	Viva Learning and Viva Insights—Viva email integration
	Viva Learning and Viva Connections—learning content in Viva Connections

Free LinkedIn Learning Courses

The following courses have (Table 6-2) been made available free of charge and does not require a LinkedIn Enterprise license, or a Viva Learning Premium subscription:

Table 6-2. *Free LinkedIn business courses*

Title A-K	Title L-Z
Balancing Work and Life as a Work-from-Home Parent	Leading Remote Projects and Virtual Teams
Bill George on Self Awareness, Authenticity, and Leadership	Managing Projects with Microsoft Teams
Building Relationships While Working from Home	Microsoft Teams Tips and Tricks
Building Self-Confidence	Microsoft Viva Essential Training
Common Meeting Problems	Microsoft Viva First Look
Communicating Nonverbally	Nir Eyal on Creating Habit-Forming Products
Communicating with Charisma	Online Searching Tips and Tricks

(continued)

Table 6-2. (*continued*)

Title A-K	Title L-Z
Communication within Teams	Organizing Your Remote Office for Maximum Productivity
Defining and Achieving Professional Goals	PowerPoint: Animating Text and Objects for Beginners
Difficult Conversations: Talking About Race at Work	Privacy in the New World of Work
Digital Strategy	Python Code Challenges
Excel Quick Tips	Shane Snow on Dream Teams
Excel: You Can Do This	Skills for Inclusive Conversations
Find a Job in the Hidden Job Market	Team Collaboration in Office 365 (Microsoft 365)
Gretchen Rubin on Creating Great Workplace Habits	Teamwork Foundations
How to be an Adaptable Employee During Change and Uncertainty	Time Management Tips
Inclusive Leadership	Travel Hacks: Staying Productive on the Road
iOS and iPad OS: iPhone and iPad Essential Training	Windows Quick Tips
Jodi Glickman on Make 'Em Love You at Work'	Word Quick Tips

Table 6-3. *Free LinkedIn creative courses*

Title A-L	Title L-Z
Banish Your Inner Critic to Unleash Creativity	Learning Premiere Pro
Getting Started in User Experience	Lightroom: Get Professional Results
Illustrator Quick Start	Marketing to Humans
iMovie 10.1.8 Essential Training	Photographing for Compositing in Photoshop
Learning Audacity	Simple Photo Edits On Your Phone
Learning Graphic Design: Presentations	Social Media Video for Business and Marketing

Table 6-4. *Free LinkedIn tech courses*

Title A-L	Title M-Z
Android Development Essential Training: Your First App with Kotlin	Microsoft Enterprise Mobility Suite: Management and Security
Building a Home IT Lab	Office 365 for Administrators: Troubleshooting Issues for Users
Building Your First iOS 13 App	Python: Programming Efficiently
CSS: Advanced Layouts with Grid	Remote Collaboration for Developers with Microsoft Live Share
Data Visualization Best Practices	SQL Code Challenges
Design a Cloud Migration Strategy	Succeeding in Web Development: Full Stack and Front End
DJ Patil: Ask Me Anything	Tech Sense
GitHub Quick Tip	Technology and Design Ethics
Implementing a Vulnerability Management Program	Visual Studio Code Productivity Tips
Installing Apache, MySQL, and PHP	Visual Studio Step-by-Step
Learning Java Applications	WordPress: Creating an Intranet Website
Learning Swift Playgrounds Application Development	

Table 6-5. *Free LinkedIn skills courses*

Title
Learn LinkedIn Sales Navigator
Learning LinkedIn Recruiter
LinkedIn Quick Tips
Rock Your LinkedIn Profile

Roles

As a Global, SharePoint or Microsoft Teams Admin, you can configure settings necessary for Viva Learning. A new role has been made available specifically for Knowledge Admins to administer the content and licensing in your organization for Viva Learning.

Adding the Knowledge Admin

1. Go to Roles and select Role assignments in the Microsoft 365 admin center (Figure 6-1).

2. Under the Azure AD tab, select Knowledge Administrator.

3. Select "Assigned admins," and then select "Add."

4. Select the person you choose for the role, and then select "Add."

To remove a Knowledge Administrator, you would follow the same steps, select the admin name, and "Remove."

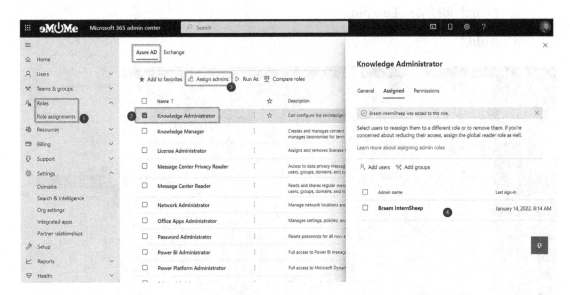

Figure 6-1. *Assign the Knowledge Administrator role*

Set Up Microsoft Viva Learning

The Viva Learning app is allowed, by default for all the Microsoft Teams users in your company. As mentioned, with your Microsoft Teams license as part of your Microsoft/ Office 365 subscription, you have access to some of the features, without purchasing the premium subscription. Refer to the Free Viva Learning paragraph.

Pin the Viva Learning App for Employees

Although the app is available for all employees to search and pin to their Microsoft Teams app bar, as admin, you can add the app to your Global (org-wide default) policy. This will pin the app automatically for all employees. Follow these steps to pin the app (Figure 6-2):

1. In the Microsoft Teams admin center, under Teams apps, navigate to "Setup policies."

2. Select the policy you want to apply this to (or create a new policy) then click on "Add apps."

3. Search for "Viva Learning."

4. "Add."

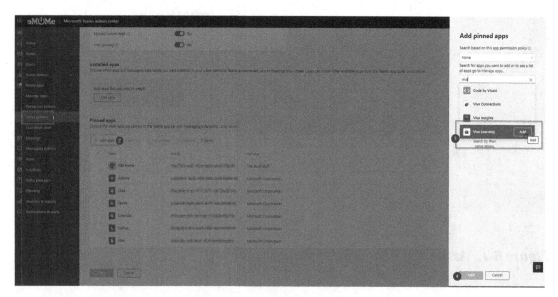

Figure 6-2. *Add the Viva Learning app to a Policy*

Once the app is added, you can

1. Select the app.

2. "Move it up or down," based on your requirement.

3. "Save" your changes (See Figure 6-3 below):

Figure 6-3. *Move the app into position on the Teams App Bar*

Block the Viva Learning App

If you need to remove the app, you will have to do so in the Teams Admin Center. Figure 6-4 illustrates how easy this is:

1. In the Microsoft Teams Admin Center, go to Teams apps, then Manage apps.

2. Search for Viva Learning.

3. Select the app.

4. Block.

Figure 6-4. *Allow or block your Viva Learning app*

Configure Your Learning Sources

As a Global or Knowledge Admin, you can configure the learning sources available in Viva Learning. Figure 6-5 shows you how:

1. In the Admin Center, go to Settings, Org Settings (if Settings does not show, click on "Show All" to expand).

2. Under the Services Tab, select Viva Learning.

3. The panel will open on the right for you to select the content sources.

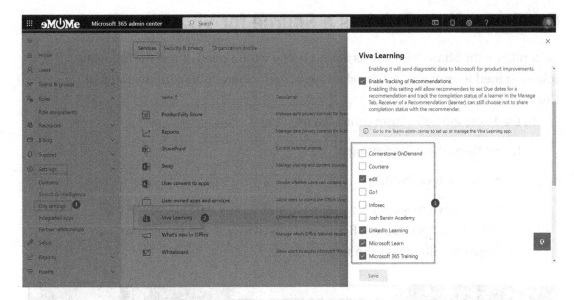

Figure 6-5. *Choose your learning sources*

Note   Microsoft Learn, Microsoft 365 Training, and LinkedIn Learning can be surfaced without the Premium license. However, the full libraries will not be available for LinkedIn Learning without an enterprise subscription with the 3rd party.

SharePoint as a Content Source

For me, the ability to add our own content through SharePoint is one of the greatest benefits of Viva Learning. Most companies create their own training content as well, whether it be PowerPoint presentations, Word documents, and even Videos.

The following document types are supported:

- Word, PowerPoint, Excel, PDF

- Audio (.m4a)

- Video (.mov, .mp4, .avi)

Configure SharePoint as a Source for Viva Learning

To configure the SharePoint site as a source, you would need one of the following roles assigned to your name: Global administrator, SharePoint administrator, or Knowledge admin.

In the Microsoft 365 admin center, go to

1. Settings, then Org Settings.

2. Select Viva Learning.

3. Scroll down to SharePoint, select it, and supply the URL where the "Learning App Content Repository" list will be built, then "Save." Figure 6-6 illustrates the steps to do so.

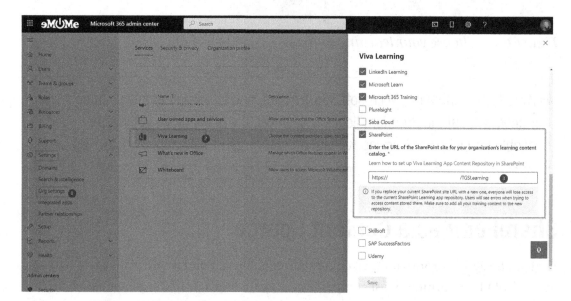

Figure 6-6. *Create the Learning App Content Repository'*

Note   The content sources do not have to be stored on the same SharePoint site collection, but can be surfaced from across your company's SharePoint site collections. You would, however, need to be a Site Owner of the site referenced for the repository. For Multi-geo clients, the preceding site URL would have to belong to the original Microsoft 365 central location. This applies to the folders reference for training content as well. Should you add folders which do not belong to the central location, you will receive an error.

Once saved, navigate to the site you specified. In site contents, you will see the Learning App Content Repository that was created (Figure 6-7):

	Contents	Subsites			

	Name	Type	Items	Modified
	Documents	Document library	13	1/13/2022 9:27 AM
	Form Templates	Document library	0	1/13/2022 9:13 AM
	Style Library	Document library	0	12/11/2021 4:42 PM
	Learning App Content Reposit	List	1	1/13/2022 9:26 AM
	Events	Events list	0	12/11/2021 4:42 PM
	Site Pages	Page library	1	12/11/2021 4:42 PM

Figure 6-7. *Learning App Content Repository in Site Contents*

Prepare the Source Material

For the best experience in the Viva Learning app, the following suggestion is made for the libraries where you store your training content. The default metadata from your library is automatically surfaced in Viva Learning by the Microsoft Graph API (modified date, created by, document name, etc).

By adding an additional Description column, it supplies Viva Learning with more information regarding the content. If not supplied, Viva Learning will simply state that the content comes from your own SharePoint libraries.

To add the description column (Figure 6-8)

1. Click on Add column and select Single line of text.

2. Give the column the name "Description" and Save.

3. You can now add folders with content to reference.

Viva Learning follows the same permission "rules" as SharePoint. An employee will not be able to use content for which they do not have the correct permission levels.

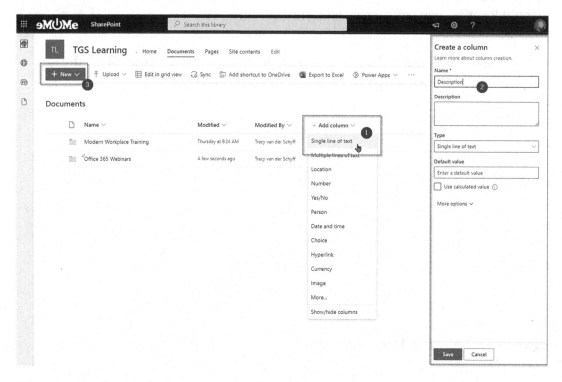

Figure 6-8. *Create the Description column*

If you receive an error that the column already exists, follow these steps first before trying to create the column again (Figure 6-9):

1. Click on the Settings Gear.

2. Go to Library Settings.

3. Click on the Description column to open, and delete it.

Figure 6-9. *Delete existing Description column*

Reference the Source Material

Now that the Learning App Content Repository exists, you can reference different sources for training content. First you must copy the URLs (Figure 6-10) from the various folders you would like to reference:

1. Click on the ellipses (…).

2. Select Copy link.

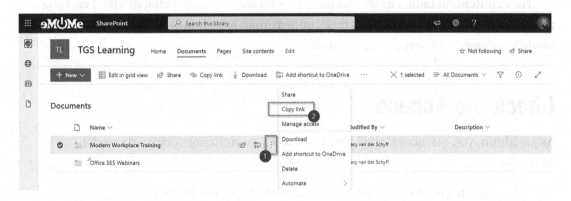

Figure 6-10. *Copy the folder URL*

Navigate to the Learning App Content Repository list built when you added the URL in the Admin Center.

1. Click on New.

2. Add the name that describes the content in that folder best and add the URL, then Save.

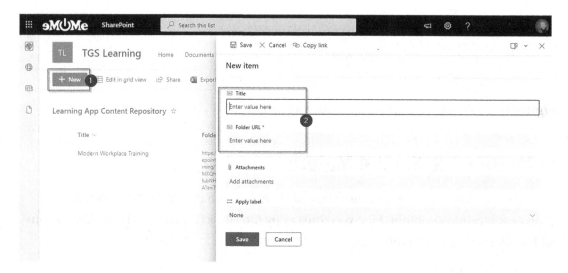

Figure 6-11. *Create a New Content Source item*

New content metadata as well as permissions are made available in Viva Learning through the *Learning Service.* This takes approximately 24 hours and applies to changes made to content and permissions as well.

Check the Access

As an admin, you can access the Learning App Content Repository in Microsoft Teams by

1. Clicking on the ellipses (…) in the top right corner of the app.

2. Select Settings.

3. Select Permissions.

4. Then clicking on Check Access.

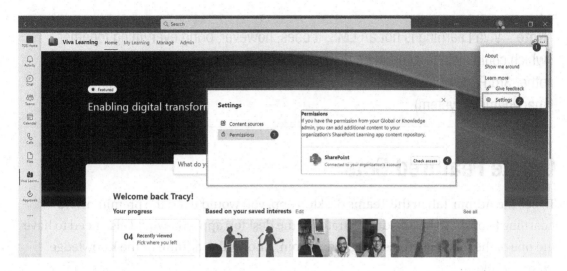

Figure 6-12. *Viva Learning App settings*

Configure the Tracking of Recommended Content

Employees and Managers can recommend content to others. If you would like to allow the recommender to set due dates and track the progress, this needs to be configured on the Admin Center. Follow the steps in Figure 6-13:

1. In the Admin Center, go to Settings, Org Settings.

2. Under the Services Tab, select Viva Learning.

3. The panel will open on the right for you to "Enable Tracking of Recommendations."

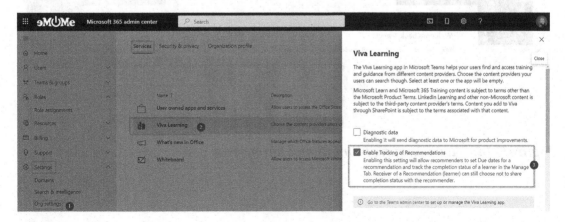

Figure 6-13. *Enable Tracking of Recommendations*

Note   Viva Learning is not an LMS, it does, however, bring everything together, which could include internal content, Microsoft 365 Training, LinkedIn Learning, other 3rd Party providers as well as (where applicable) your LMS (learning management system).

Create Featured Sets

To see the Admin Tab in the Teams desktop app, you would need the premium Viva Learning license. To be an administrator in the desktop app, you would also need to have the one of the following roles assigned: Admin, Knowledge admin, or the Knowledge Manager role.

Here administrators can create featured sets, think of these as spotlights for specific courses you would like to promote. A maximum of six courses can be added to a featured set. These will be displayed to all employees as banners which will rotate automatically, but can also be flipped through by using the arrows on the left or right. Figure 6-14 shows the promotional banner:

Figure 6-14. *Viva Learning promotional banners*

In Figure 6-15, you will see the Admin Tab in the Viva Learning app in Microsoft Teams:

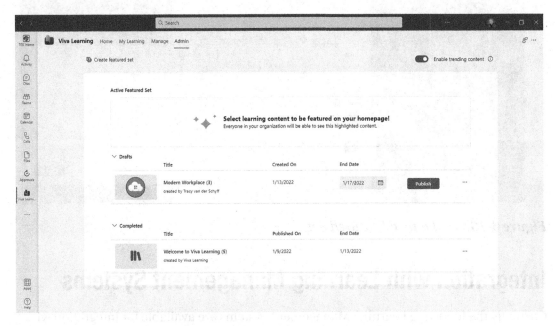

Figure 6-15. *Admin Tab in the Microsoft Teams desktop app*

To add a new featured set, you would need to (see Figure 6-16):

1. Be in the Admin tab in Viva Learning.

2. Click on Create featured set.

3. Add a name for this feature set.

4. Add the end date for the "campaign."

5. Search for the courses you would like to add (maximum six)

6. Save.

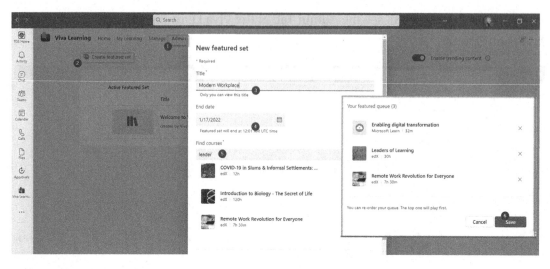

Figure 6-16. *Add a new Featured Set*

Integration with Learning Management Systems

Currently the following Learning Management Systems are available for integration with Viva Learning:

- Cornerstone OnDemand

- Saba

- SAP SuccessFactors

To add a learning management system, navigate to the Microsoft 365 Admin Center, and follow these steps in Figure 6-17:

1. Under Settings, click on Org Settings.

2. Under Services, go to Viva Learning.

3. Here you can select from the available learning management systems.

Note   Follow the technical documentation provided by Microsoft for different setup instructions per learning management system and 3rd party learning content provider.

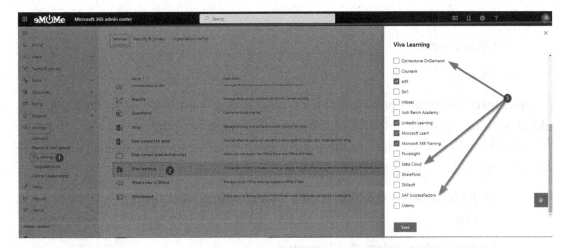

Figure 6-17. *Add your Learning Management System in the Admin Center*

Using 3rd Party Content Providers

Within Viva Learning, some content sources are free and do not require a premium license. These include Microsoft Learn, Microsoft 365 Training, and LinkedIn Learning (select courses).

Additional 3rd party content providers can be added and would then require a premium Viva Learning license (as well as the subscription with the provider). Currently these learning content providers are available to add in Viva Learning:

- Coursera

- edX

- Go1

- Infosec

- Josh Bersin Academy

- Pluralsight

- Skillsoft

- Udemy

- Edcast

- Go1

- OpenSesame

- Udacity

More learning content providers and learning management systems are continually added. Monitor the Microsoft Viva Learning product page for updates.

Should you have subscriptions for any of these 3rd party providers, follow these steps to add them to Viva Learning (Figure 6-18):

1. In the Microsoft 365 admin center, under Settings, click on Org Settings.

2. Under Services, select Viva Learning.

3. Here you will see the providers that can be added.

Any source added or removed will take up to 48 hours to reflect in Viva Learning.

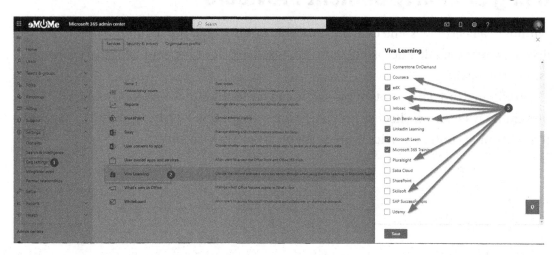

Figure 6-18. *Add your 3rd Party Content Providers*

CHAPTER 7

Viva Learning for Employees and Managers

Navigation

Pin the App in Teams

If your admin has not pinned the Viva Learning app in Microsoft Teams (see Pin the Viva Learning app for Employees for more information), you are able to do so yourself. Figure 7-1 will guide you:

1. Click on the ellipses (…).

2. Search for "Viva Learning."

3. Select the app.

4. Once loaded, right click on the app in the app bar.

5. Pin the app.

6. In the Viva Learning app Home tab, you also have the option to pin the app to the sidebar.

© D'arce Hess, Albert-Jan Schot, Tracy van der Schyff 2023
D. Hess et al., *Getting Started with Microsoft Viva*, https://doi.org/10.1007/978-1-4842-8590-9_7

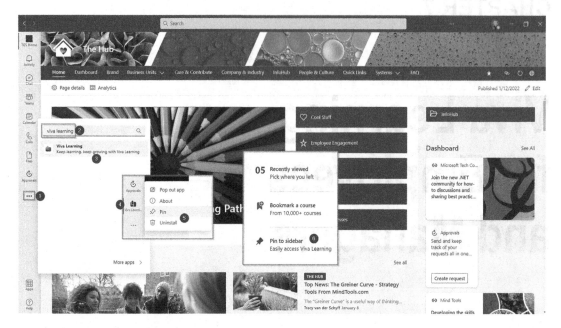

Figure 7-1. *Pin the Viva Learning app*

Show Me Around

When opening Viva Learning for the first time, you will be welcomed by the "Show me around" feature. These are text bubbles that show you around and help you become familiar with the environment.

Don't worry, if you're in a rush, you can also open it again later by clicking on the ellipses (…) in the top right corner of the app and selecting "Show me around," as seen in Figure 7-2:

Figure 7-2. *Show Me Around*

Figure 7-3 highlights an important function. We do have an impact on the technology we use and giving feedback or making suggestions is a great way to influence future changes. Click the "Give feedback" button next to the ellipsis in the top right corner to do so.

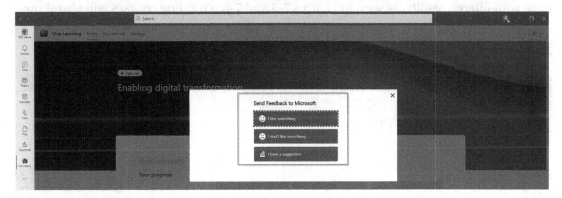

Figure 7-3. *Give Feedback*

Home Tab

In the Home tab (1) you can flip through the featured courses (2), search for courses you are interested in (3), see your recently viewed courses (4), edit your interests (5), and see your bookmarked courses (6) as seen in Figure 7-4:

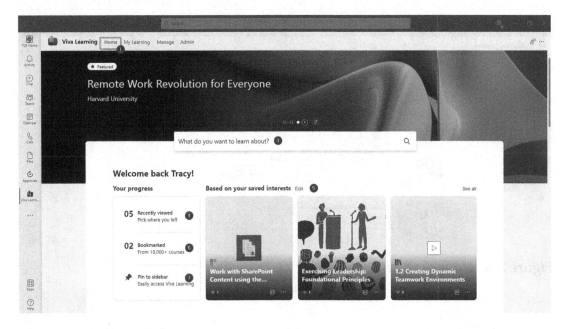

Figure 7-4. *Home Tab*

Scrolling down on the Home tab page (1), you will find the "Browse Courses" section. Here the courses are grouped by the category of "Your interests" (2); by "Providers" (3); and by "Duration" (4). Clicking on "See all" (5) will open an additional search results page with filtered results, as seen in Figures 7-5 and 7-6. Trending courses will also show on the Home tab based on learning content with more than five views during the last 30 days.

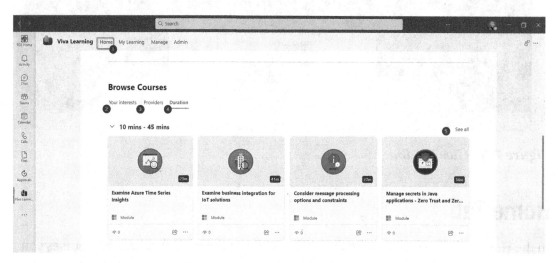

Figure 7-5. *Browse Courses*

Figure 7-6. *Using the filters*

Engaging with Your Courses

When a course has been opened under the Home tab (1), you have various options to engage and share, as seen in Figure 7-7:

1. Open the course.

2. Share (via Teams or copying the link).

3. Recommend (to a Team or person).

4. Bookmark.

5. Read information about the course.

6. Find relevant courses.

Figure 7-7.   *Engage with your Courses*

Pick Your Interests

In the Home tab (1), you will have the ability to add and edit (2) your interests (3). These interests identified (Figure 7-8), will help personalize the content you see in Viva Learning.

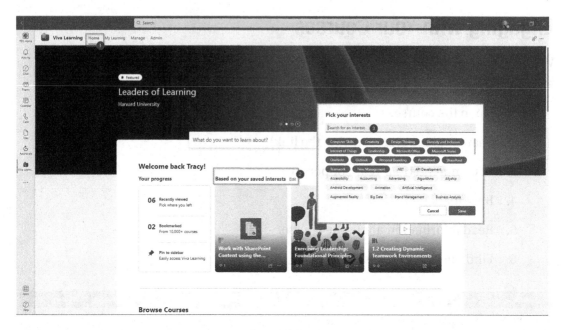

Figure 7-8. *Viva Learning Home Tab – Add Your Interests*

My Learning

Navigation

Figure 7-9 shows the "My Learning" tab (1), where you will find your "Bookmarked" courses (2), "Recommendations" (3), "Recently viewed" courses (4), and "Completed" (5). Here you can also browse for more courses (6):

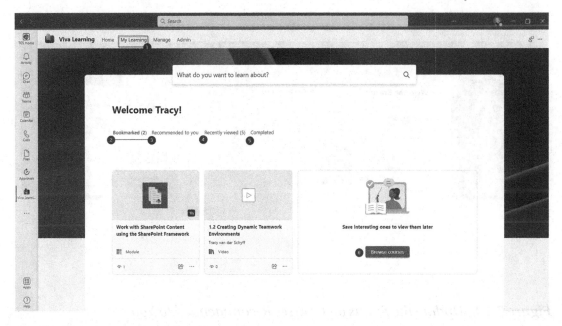

Figure 7-9. *My Learning Tab*

Courses Recommended to You

Based on the settings applied in the Admin Center (see Configure the Tracking of Recommended Content), courses recommended to you will have a due date and a status. To update the status, follow the steps in Figure 7-10.

1. Navigate to "Recommended to you."

2. Select the course you wish to update.

3. Change the status.

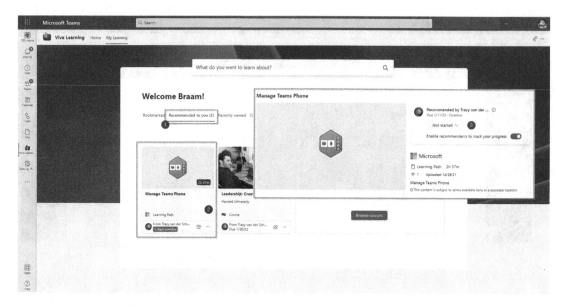

Figure 7-10. *Update the Status on Courses Recommended to You*

Recommend Courses

As a manager, you might want to recommend courses to your team members by following the steps below in Figure 7-11

1. Open the course and click on "Recommend."

2. Add the name (no more than 50 names).

3. Adding a "Note" will explain why the course is important.

4. Complete the "Due date."

5. Click on "Recommend" and the recommendation will be sent.

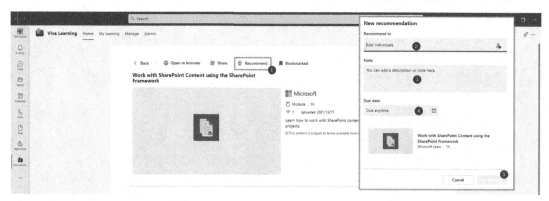

Figure 7-11. *Recommend a Course*

Sharing Courses

Sharing courses are great for "recommending" a course, without formally *assigning* it to someone. This would be used more between colleagues. In Figure 7-12 it is shown that there are two ways to share a course:

1. You can share via Teams with a person, a group, or a channel.

2. A link can be copied to share via other mediums.

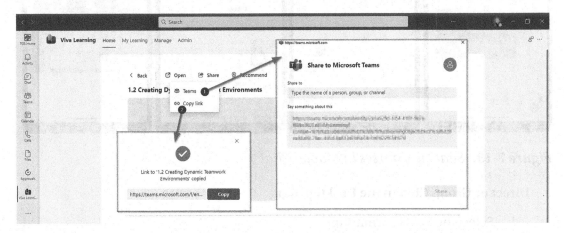

Figure 7-12. *Sharing a Course*

Embed Learning into Chat Conversations

Courses can be shared via Chat, Group Chat, and Posts in Channels in the mobile as well as desktop app. See examples in Figures 7-13–7-15:

Mobile app:

1. Select add (+).

2. Choose the Viva Learning app.

3. Search for a course.

4. Select the course.

5. Send.

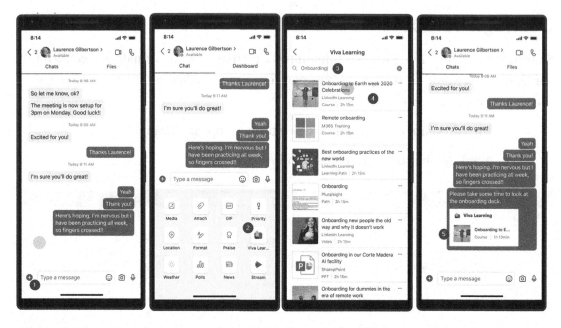

Figure 7-13. *Sharing Courses in Mobile Chat*

Direct or Group Chat in the Desktop app:

1. Select the Viva Learning app.

2. Search for a course.

Figure 7-14. *Sharing Courses in Desktop Chat*

Posts in a Teams Channel in the Desktop app:

1. Select the Viva Learning app.

2. Search for a course.

3. Select the course.

Figure 7-15. *Sharing Courses in Desktop Channel Posts*

Manage

Manage Courses Recommended to Others

Under the Manage tab, you will see courses you have recommended to others. If the tracking has been switched on (see Configure the Tracking of Recommended Content), you will be able to see the course "Title," "Created on," "Due date," "Recommended to" as well as the "Recommendation details." Figure 7-16 shows the "Recommendation details" button, which will show the status of the recommendation:

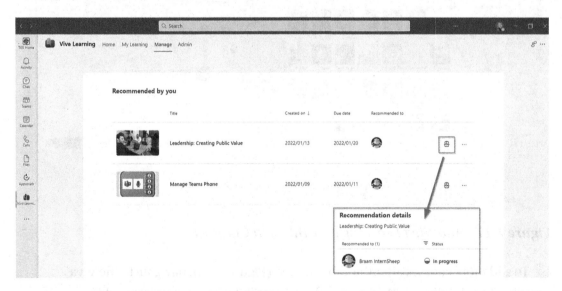

Figure 7-16. *Recommendation Details*

Add Viva Learning as a Tab to Your Teams

When working closely with a group of people in a Microsoft Team, it could add value to add Viva Learning as a Tab on a Channel. Follow the steps in Figure 7-17 to add Viva Learning and select courses to show:

1. Add the Tab (+).

2. Select (or search for) Viva Learning.

3. Give the Tab a name.

4. Search for courses you would like to add.

5. You can select multiple courses.

6. Save.

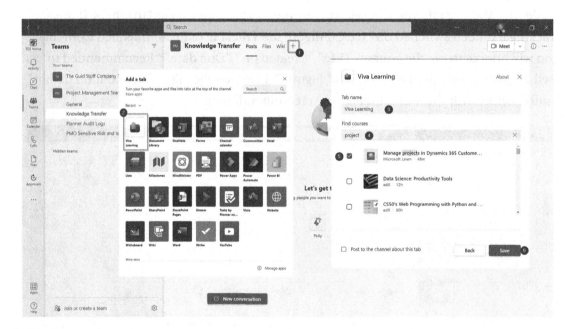

Figure 7-17. *Add Viva Learning as a Tab on a Channel*

To add more courses after the Tab is added (Figure 7-18), navigate to the Viva Learning Tab (1), click on "Add new" (2), and search for more courses to add:

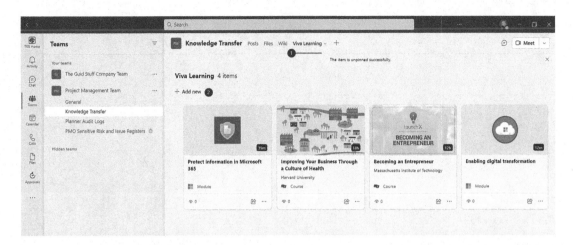

Figure 7-18. *Add additional Courses to your Tab*

To remove courses (Figure 7-19) after the Tab has been added, click on the ellipses on the course (1) and "Unpin" (2) the course.

Figure 7-19. *Remove Courses*

Closing

Empowering those around me has always been the driving force in my life. Now, with Viva Learning, it becomes easier to change company cultures and help employees evolve into lifelong, self-learners. I hope you'll enjoy using Viva Learning and see the benefit of empowering yourself, as well as those around you. Always keep in mind that products do not fix problems, people fix problems with products – using Viva Learning can only be as successful as the change management campaign that accompanies it, and the necessary management support.

PART III

Microsoft Viva Connections

Viva Connections brings the workplace together and becomes the gateway to all the resources your employees need in their digital workplace, including news, videos, company documents, communities as well as other relevant information.

CHAPTER 8

The Intranet

The Purpose of an Intranet

As much as technology has given us the ability to be closer to one another, regardless of physical distance, the impact of remote working had the opposite effect. More employees are feeling disengaged now than ever before, despite sitting on more online meetings per day and being trapped by the "always on era."

Traditionally, Intranets were deployed in companies as a central storage for policies, procedures, forms, etc. as well as a platform to confirm brand, build culture, communicate with employees, and share relevant information and access to processes (Figure 8-1).

Figure 8-1. *Purpose of an Intranet*

© D'arce Hess, Albert-Jan Schot, Tracy van der Schyff 2023
D. Hess et al., *Getting Started with Microsoft Viva*, https://doi.org/10.1007/978-1-4842-8590-9_8

The Intelligent Intranet

Communication Sites in SharePoint Online allows us to design and build beautiful, modern Intranet portals and with guidance from the SharePoint Look Book it is easier than ever, for citizen developers to do so.

This **Intelligent Intranet** delivers a **personalized** experience, engages and informs the entire organization, connects employees, and gives them access to the tools and content they need, **relevant** to them, **when** they need it, **how** and **where** they want to engage with it.

The Challenge

The workplace consists of many apps and services that deliver the preceding content. In the past, employees would have to navigate to different websites and use various tools. The frustration created by the confusion of "too many apps, too many places" created opportunities for "shadow IT" to thrive. Microsoft Teams was the first step toward uniting the workplace tools and paved the way for the Viva modules to further optimize and eventually deliver the integrated employee experience platform (EXP).

CHAPTER 9

Introduction to Microsoft Viva Connections

Microsoft Viva Connections Overview

No longer is the Intranet your single point of entry, no longer just a "place," but rather an experience. Viva Connections brings it all together and becomes the gateway to all the resources your employees need in their digital workplace, including news, videos, company documents, communities as well as other relevant information. Viva Connections delivers a customizable app in Microsoft Teams desktop as well as mobile. Figure 9-1 shares a glimpse of what you can expect.

© D'arce Hess, Albert-Jan Schot, Tracy van der Schyff 2023
D. Hess et al., *Getting Started with Microsoft Viva*, https://doi.org/10.1007/978-1-4842-8590-9_9

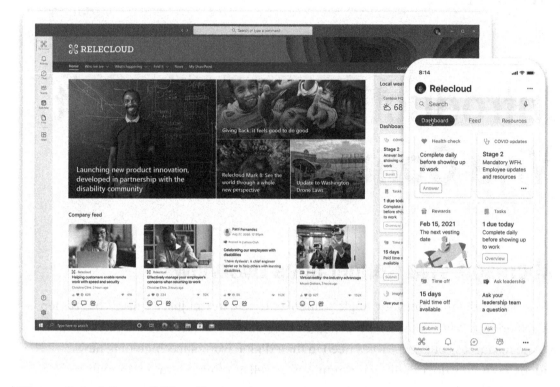

Figure 9-1. *Microsoft Viva Connections*

Integration with Microsoft 365 Apps

Viva Connections enables companies to identify their Intranets as Home Sites and surface these inside of Microsoft Teams. It provides a single-entry point for employee engagement and internal communications. The integration with other Microsoft 365 apps allows for a rich communication and engagement experience (Figure 9-2).

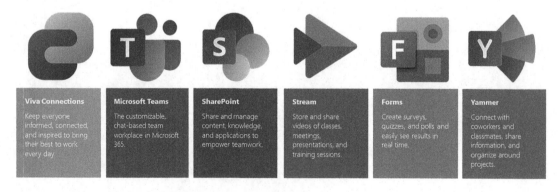

Figure 9-2. *Microsoft 365 apps integration*

Core Concepts and Capabilities

Viva Connections is available as a mobile and desktop experience which allow users to stay in touch, up-to-date, and informed, whether they are at home, at the office, or in the field.

With common concepts and capabilities (Figure 9-3), it delivers a smooth transitioning for users to have the same experience and access to resources, information, and business processes across platforms. As one of the modules in the Microsoft Viva Family, Connections is built on **Microsoft 365**, powered by **SharePoint**, and made accessible through **Microsoft Teams**.

Although I have placed a lot of emphasis on the Intranet, Viva Connections delivers so much more. On both the desktop and mobile apps, you will have access to the Global Navigation (Resources), the Dashboard as well as a personalized Feed.

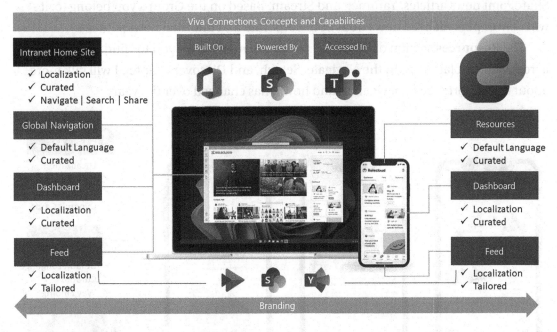

Figure 9-3. *Microsoft Viva Connections Concepts and Capabilities*

In the next couple of paragraphs, I will share more information on what to expect from the desktop and mobile experience, as well as "good to know" tips and tricks on the preceding concepts and capabilities.

The Mobile Experience

Microsoft Teams has become the core to the ecosystem that supports our modern workplace. As Viva Connections is surfaced inside of your mobile Microsoft Teams app, it becomes part of your toolset and not "just another app." Inside the app (Figure 9-4), you will notice three focus areas: Dashboard, Feed, and Resources.

The **Dashboard** is created by an administrator in SharePoint for the company and tailored to suit all employees using target audiences. It is compiled of dynamic cards which supply the relevant tools needed. Think of these as "buttons" to the apps, sites, and information you use regularly.

See more about this in the Create and Customize your Dashboard section of the Preparation and Setup chapter.

The purpose of the **Feed** is to keep you up-to-date with the latest news from SharePoint news articles, Yammer, and Stream. Based on the Groups you belong to, it will deliver personalized news from both corporate and informal news sources.

The **Resources** section delivers the navigation needed, for you to "find your way" across various platforms. In the Navigate, Search, and Discover chapter, I will talk more about the importance of navigation and how it has changed over the years.

Figure 9-4. *Microsoft Viva Connections Mobile Experience*

The Desktop Experience

As with the mobile experience, the Viva Connections app also displays in the Microsoft Teams desktop app. This is where the real work happens for me and having access to my content, chats, calendar, tasks, AND my Intranet in one place, is a big win. See Figure 9-5 for an overview of the desktop capabilities.

In the Way Finding section, I talk about the importance of finding what you need, where you are. This is where Viva Connections inside of Microsoft Teams add even more value. We can now **Navigate** across sites and resources, **Search** in the Microsoft Teams search box for Intranet content and even **Share** Intranet content in Teams – without ever leaving the Teams desktop app.

The same **Dashboard** that is visible on your mobile app can be added as a web part to your home page. If you do not have space on your home page, you could simply add the link to the Dashboard in your navigation or as a Quick Link button on the page.

Apart from the News that displays in the SharePoint app bar (Global Navigation), you can also add the "**My Feed**" web part to the home page, which will be personalized and show the current user what is likely to be most relevant to them.

Figure 9-5. Microsoft Viva Connections Desktop Experience

Curated vs. Tailored Experiences

The experience in Viva Connections is achieved by using curated as well as tailored content. It is important to know the difference as it will help you plan your environment to suit different audiences.

Curated – Carefully chosen and thoughtfully organized or presented

Tailored – Made or changed especially to be suitable for a particular situation or purpose (person)

The Home site (home page) will be built by a site owner(s) who makes the decisions regarding web parts to use, pages to build, etc. Although it should be done with the input from the various stakeholders, it is still considered curated. This applies to the Dashboard as well as Resources (Navigation). You can, however, use audience targeting to hide specific web parts, dashboard cards, or navigation links based on permissions. Only the Feed is tailored as it will display content relevant to the current user. See Table 9-1 for a summary.

Table 9-1. *Curated vs. Tailored details*

Capability Name	Curated vs. Tailored	How
Home site	Curated	Author controls layout, web parts, and audience targeting of content.
Dashboard	Curated	Author selects cards to show and uses AAD groups to target them to specific audiences.
Feed	Tailored	Content is automatically prioritized and displayed based on signals associated with content from SharePoint and Yammer posts.
Resources	Curated	Using AAD groups, menu items in the global navigation can be targeted to specific audiences.

Language

Also called "localization," Viva Connections allows for the translation of English content into (currently) 27 languages. The Dashboard and Feed can be translated into the user's preferred language, but the Resources (Global Navigation) will be displayed in the tenant's default language.

CHAPTER 10

Preparation and Setup

In this chapter, we will cover the necessary steps on your journey of discovering how greater employee engagement and connectivity can foster healthier company cultures and improved employee well-being. Areas covered (as seen in Figure 10-1) will be

1. Intranet

2. Home Site

3. Global Navigation

4. Dashboards

5. Feed

6. Application

7. Policies

8. Change Management

© D'arce Hess, Albert-Jan Schot, Tracy van der Schyff 2023
D. Hess et al., *Getting Started with Microsoft Viva*, https://doi.org/10.1007/978-1-4842-8590-9_10

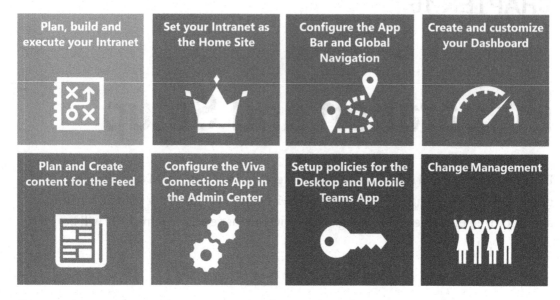

Figure 10-1. *Microsoft Viva Connections step-by-step instructions*

Intranet Groundwork

As explained in Chapter 1, your Intranet plays an integral role in the integrated employee experience. If your Intranet has existed on SharePoint for some time, now would be the time to consider a refresh and update. The following are some considerations:

1. An Intranet audit will assist in making decisions on

   a. Relevance of content and resources referenced

   b. Flow of information and navigation

   c. Content owners and permissions

   d. Focus areas and purpose

   e. Strategic alignment to current company culture and objectives

   f. Default language and preferences

2. Are there any sites or pages that should be transformed into the modern experience? Only modern pages and sites can open in the Microsoft Teams client.

3. Is it time for a rebrand? Microsoft has incredible resources
    available to inspire and guide you. Go through the examples and
    templates in the SharePoint Look Book. Also keep in mind that
    you can create and use your own custom color themes in you
    SharePoint sites.

If you do not have an Intranet yet, you are in luck. It has never been easier to plan
and build a beautiful, intelligent Intranet with out-of-the-box features, no development
required. Trust me, I am a citizen developer, and Microsoft has empowered me to deliver
many beautiful Intranets.

Define the Home Site

A Home Site is required by Viva Connections as it will be identified and used as the
landing page/site which will be displayed in Microsoft Teams. Although it does not
have to be your Intranet, it needs to be a Communication Site template and it would be
advised to pick a site with significant business purpose, high value, and site traffic. My
preference would be the Intranet, but could be any site that brings together necessary
content, resources, and sites. It is vital that everyone in the organization should have
access to this site; this can be achieved by applying changes in your site's permission
settings.

A site can be identified as the Home Site by using PowerShell or applying changes in
the SharePoint Admin Center.

Using the SharePoint Admin Center

Navigate to the SharePoint Admin Center ➤ Settings ➤ Select Home Site and enter the
URL to the site you have identified as the Home Site. After a couple of minutes, the Home
Site URL will appear on the Settings page in the Current Value column. See Figure 10-2
for guidance:

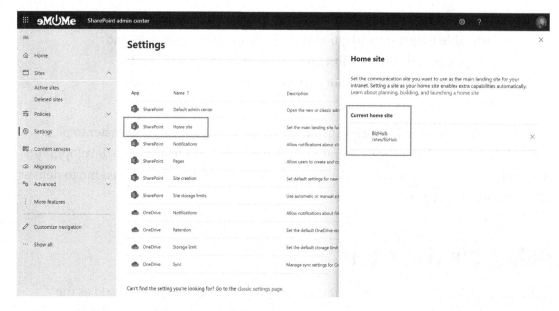

Figure 10-2. *Set the Viva Connections Home Site in the Admin Center*

Using PowerShell

Using the SharePoint Online Management Shell, connect to SharePoint as a Global Admin or SharePoint Admin. Once authenticated and connected, you will run the below cmdlet to set the specified URL as the Home Site.

```
Set-SPOHomeSite -HomeSiteUrl <siteUrl>
```

Navigate, Search, and Discover

To understand the significance and value of the SharePoint App Bar and other Microsoft 365 improvements, I would like to first share some insights on "The Evolution of Finding Stuff."

The Evolution of Finding Stuff

Over the last couple of years, I have authored many articles on digital literacy and how, without the necessary training and awareness campaigns, we cannot fully realize the benefit of the exponential improvements we are experiencing in technology.

For example, when Delve (codename Oslo) was launched in 2014, most users were afraid of the "dashboard" that suddenly displayed information that they had not navigated to or searched for. Many companies asked to remove the app from the app launcher, rather than informing and training their users.

In its simplest form, our evolution should have taken the following path, as seen in Figure 10-3:

- Saving items on our desktops, to find it again (**See**)

- Navigating through website and pc menus and nested folders (**Navigate**)

- Searching for files, settings, and programs rather than navigating (**Search**)

- Finding content where and when it matters (**Discovery**)

In January 2007, with the launch of Windows Vista, Microsoft made a significant update to the Windows Start Menu. No longer only available to navigate to settings, files, and programs, you could now also hit the Windows key on your keyboard and just start typing, to search your PC.

I meet end users every single day, who still save all their files on their desktops and navigate through menus and nested folders. Most of them have never used the Windows Button on their keyboards. The "/files" command in the Command Bar and the incredibly powerful search across Teams, Channels, Files, and Chat in Microsoft Teams are more great examples.

Note   Without efficient change management, technology will become an obstacle, not a helper, due to users continuing on old paths with outdated habits.

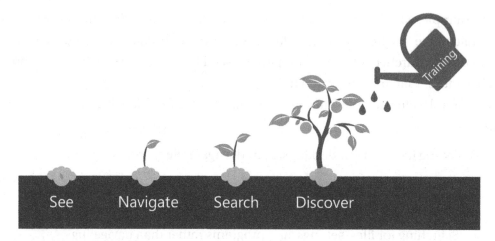

Figure 10-3. *The Evolution of Finding Stuff*

Global Way Finding

Although not a new concept, using the term "**way finding**" (Figure 10-4) when referring to navigating digital (virtual) environments is a new way of thinking. As signposts are a form of communication, the "Three Cs of Effective Communication" would also apply:

- Clear

- Concise

- Consistent

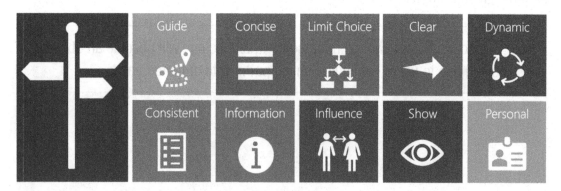

Figure 10-4. *Global Way Finding*

Historically, wayfinding refers to the techniques used by travelers over land and sea to find relatively unmarked and often mislabeled routes.

—Wikipedia

Way finding is therefore a system "we use" when we design systems and navigation to support and influence our users in their decision-making. It is about supplying relevant information, tailored to the audience, to help them get to where they need to be.

Configure Your Navigation

The SharePoint app bar as seen in Figure 10-5, improves our ability to empower our users to find content, information, solutions, and resources wherever they are in the SharePoint. It dynamically displays frequent and followed SharePoint sites (including those behind your Microsoft Teams), security trimmed files, news posts, and now also your recent and favorite Microsoft Lists. The app bar can be found on the left-hand side in SharePoint (including the SharePoint Home Page). As you can see in Figure 3-11, the following information and content is displayed:

1. 🏠 The 1st icon expands your Global Navigation from your Home Site (Intranet).

2. 🌐 The 2nd icon will list the SharePoint sites.

3. 🗔 The 3rd icon delivers the latest news posts to your fingertips.

4. 🗋 The 4th icon displays your files.

5. 🎛 The 5th icon shows your recent as well as favorite Microsoft Lists.

Figure 10-5. *The SharePoint app bar's Personalized Content*

Note Where relevant, all content, news, and information will always be security trimmed, based on your permissions.

The SharePoint App Bar and Global Navigation

Once your site has been identified and configured as the Home Site, you will see the "Global Navigation" option under Settings. Here you will enable the Global Navigation, supply the logo to be used in the SharePoint app bar (transparent PNG of 20x20 pixels), add the title to be displayed and choose Home or Hub navigation. Follow the steps in Figure 10-6:

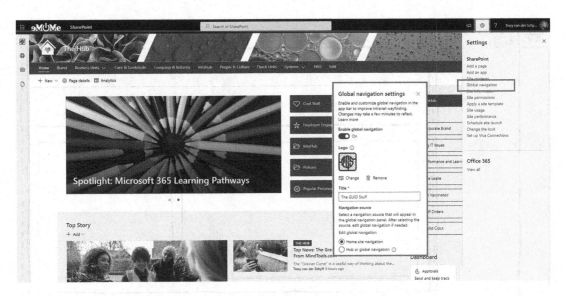

Figure 10-6. *Configure the SharePoint app bar and Global Navigation*

There are three different ways to display your Home Site and Hub navigation:

1. **Option 1:** Display both the Hub Navigation and the Home Site Navigation on the Home Page, and then set the Home Site Navigation to show in the SharePoint app bar.

2. **Option 2:** Display both the Hub Navigation and the Home Site Navigation on the Home Page, and then set the Hub Navigation to show in the SharePoint app bar.

3. **Option 3:** Display the Hub Navigation only on the Home Page and the Home Site Navigation in the SharePoint app bar.

Figure 10-7 will help you identify the areas:

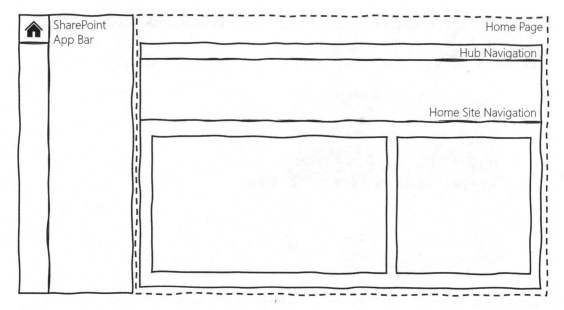

Figure 10-7. *SharePoint Global Navigation and app bar*

Note   Keep in mind that if the specific Home Site Navigation is set to display in the SharePoint app bar, it will do so across SharePoint/any other SharePoint site you might navigate to. The current site will still display on the Home Page of that site. Always refer to the Microsoft articles for up-to-date notes and considerations regarding the impact new features could have on site and page customizations.

Create and Customize Your Dashboard

Now that you have your Intranet, it has been set as the Home Site and you have set up the Global Navigation, we are ready to look at the Dashboard.

Building the Dashboard was much easier than I thought it would be as it can be built with no code. A developer is only required if you require custom cards.

Create Your Dashboard

To start creating your Dashboard, go to the Home Site, Settings gear, Setup Viva Connections and then select "Create Dashboard" (Figure 10-8).

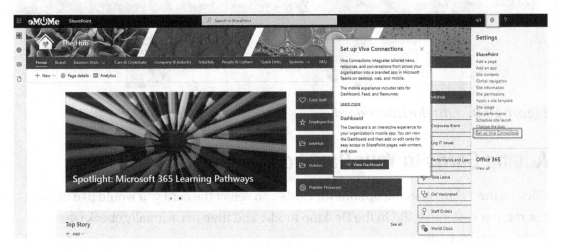

Figure 10-8. *Setup Viva Connections Dashboard*

Although it opens in Mobile view by default, you also have a Desktop view. Currently the following built-in cards are available to use:

- Approvals

- Assigned Tasks

- Card Design (for simplified custom card creation)

- Shifts

- Web Link and

- Third-party cards

- Top news card

- Viva Learning

Note   As new cards are frequently added, refer to the technical resources for configuration per card type. "URL for technical resources - `https://learn.microsoft.com/enus/viva/connections/create-dashboard`"

To start adding cards to you Dashboard select the "Edit," as shown in the Figure 10-9:

Figure 10-9. *Edit the Dashboard*

Adding Cards to Your Dashboard

Click on the "+" to open the options for cards and select the card you would like to use. For me, it is easier to build in the Desktop mode, and then occasionally check what the Mobile view looks like.

Figure 10-10. *Adding cards to your Dashboard*

Configuring the Cards for Your Dashboard

If you are creating the dashboard, the chances are good that you are a site owner who was involved in building the site. Adding cards on this page is the same as adding web parts on SharePoint pages and configuring them. On the left of the card, you will see the pen for edit, move, copy, and delete (Figure 10-11). The configuration will open on the right, and depending on the type of card, you would need to complete the details, supply images, etc.

Warning   Do not Publish (top right) the page if you are not ready for users to see it. Save a draft (top left) until you are ready.

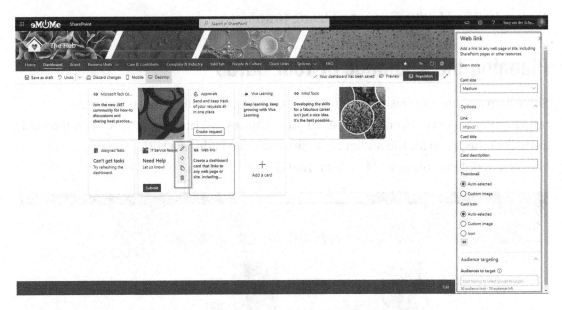

Figure 10-11. *Modifying the properties on your cards*

Planning the Layout of Your Dashboard

Cards can be moved into better positions after they are added (see Figure 10-12). If you want to add the Dashboard web part on your home page it will be better to plan in the Mobile view. As the web part could have many cards based on the audience, it would be best suited for the vertical column running down on the right-hand side of your Home Page.

Tip   Consider changing cards sizes to "Large" and adding catchy images.

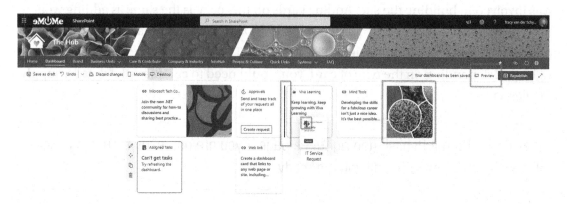

Figure 10-12. *Moving Cards and Using Graphics*

Planning the Audience of Your Cards

Since there is only one Dashboard for your company, the ability to use audience targeting comes in very handy. Figure 10-13 illustrates just how easy that is. Edit the card and select the group for the audience. In this example I added a URL to a SharePoint library that only the Strategy Members should have access to.

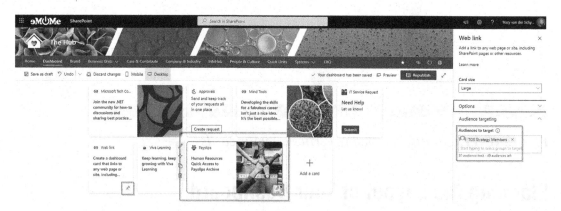

Figure 10-13. *Audience Targeting on Cards*

When using audience targeting, it is even more important to test it. In the Preview mode, you can select the audience you would like to test. Once selected, it will only show the cards restricted to that audience, and the cards with no restrictions on. In Figure 10-14, you will see the Available Audiences shown based on target audiences that have been set up on cards already.

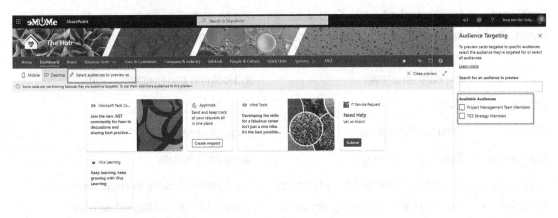

Figure 10-14. *Select Audience to Preview As*

Access the Dashboard

By default, your Dashboard (once published) is available in the Microsoft Teams Mobile app as one of the three tabs: Dashboard; Feed, and Resources. If added as a web part (Dashboard for Viva Connections) on the Home Page, it will also be displayed in the Microsoft Teams Desktop app on your identified Home Page. As the Dashboard has its own URL, a great idea would be to add it to your Global Navigation as well for quick access (see Figure 10-15).

For more information on editing your site/global navigation, see Set up global navigation in the SharePoint app bar.

Although designed for a consistent experience across Desktop and Mobile, there are small differences which can be noted in Table 10-1.

Table 10-1. *The Dashboard in mobile vs. desktop view*

Element	Mobile	Desktop
Dashboard	Displays as the default tab in the Viva Connections app in Teams.	Can be added to your home site as a web part.
Dashboard layout	Fixed in portrait mode. Card sizes can be medium (which shows two cards on one row) or large (which shows one card on a row).	Can be portrait or landscape with varying numbers of cards on each row depending on whether the web part is used in a 1-, 2-, or 3-column page section layout.
Card UI	Native	HTML based
Card order	Same as in Desktop	Same as in Mobile
Card reflow	Same as in Desktop	Same as in Mobile
How many cards are shown	All cards without audience targeting plus audience-targeted cards where the viewer is part of the targeted audience.	The number of cards to show can be specified in the Dashboard web part settings, but which cards are shown may vary depending on audience targeting.

Figure 10-15. *Access to the Dashboard*

Plan and Create Content for Your Feed

Viva Connections might be an incredible tool, but we all know that "content is king" and without up-to-date content, relevant news, and resources, your Home Site will soon be forgotten. Apart from the graphics and the actual messaging, there are some other factors to consider:

- Understanding how the Feed prioritizes and personalizes content and using that to your advantage.

- Will you be using a dedicated organizational news site or news web parts on existing sites?

- Where will your news come from, SharePoint or Yammer, or both? In my experience using both delivers a more diverse news mix, especially when considering corporate vs. informal/community type news.

- If you want to publish Video Links to the Feed, it will have to be on a SharePoint organizational news site. Embedding a Stream video on a normal News post is of course possible on any site.

- Use the Boost and Featured options in Yammer as well as the Boost feature in SharePoint to amplify and elevate your news.

Configure the Viva Connections App in the Admin Center

Our next step would be to add the Viva Connections app in the Admin Center (Figure 10-16). This would allow us to pick this app and add it to the policy in the next step.

1. Go to the Microsoft Teams Admin Center.

2. Under Teams Apps, select Manage Apps.

3. Search for Viva Connections and select the app.

4. Click on Customize for the Customize panel to open on the right.

5. Supply the short name you would like to use for the app in
    your tenant.

    a. If you do not have your own privacy and terms of use policy,
        you can leave the Microsoft default as is.

    b. Scroll down to the logo. It requires a color 192x192px logo
        for the Admin Center and then it requires a transparent
        outline icon of 32x32px that will be the home button in
        Microsoft Teams.

    c. Apply to Save.

6. Select Allow to unblock the App (can be allowed when setting up
    your policy later)

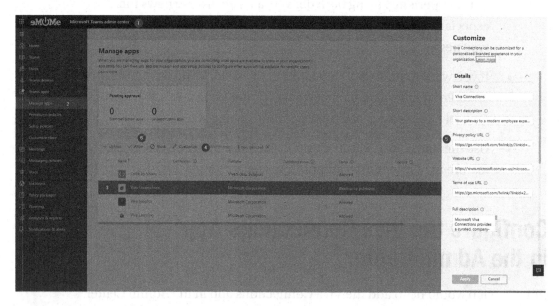

Figure 10-16. *Add the Viva Connections app*

Set Up Policies for Desktop and Mobile Teams App

Now that the app is added, we can select it to show in our policy (Figure 10-17).

1. In the Microsoft Teams Admin Center

2. Set up Policies

3. I selected my Global Policy, but you can set up a new policy should this be for specific users.

4. Add apps

5. Search for the short name you gave the app and add

6. The app will be added at the bottom, use the "Move up" button to move it to the top

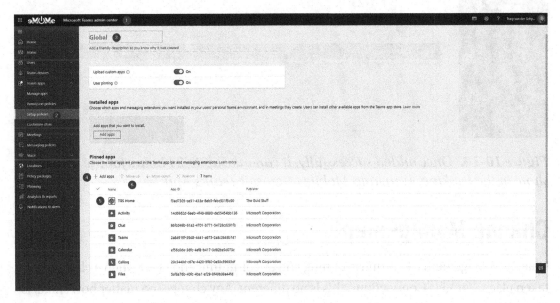

Figure 10-17. *Configure the Teams Policy*

Allow the Use of the App

In the Admin Center, the Viva Connections app is set to "Blocked by Publisher." Once you have followed the preceding steps (Figure 10-18), you can now set the status to "Allow."

1. In the Microsoft Teams Admin Center

2. Go back to Manage Apps

3. Search for the short name and select the app

4. Set the status to "Allow"

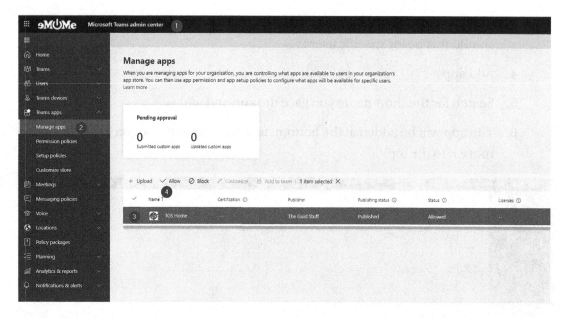

Figure 10-18. *Once added successfully, it can take up to 24 hours for the icon to show in the Desktop, Web, and Mobile Microsoft Teams App*

Change Management

Change Management can require training and or communications for when a change has taken place. For Viva Connections, this is no different. Any change, no matter how small, is disruptive to the user, especially if they do not understand the purpose of the new feature.

With all the incredible tools at your fingertips, consider a SharePoint News post with details of what to expect and the purpose 7 to 14 days before the change. Once you have launched Viva Connections, another SharePoint News post with some more information, for example a small demo video from Stream or a GIF image with some quick tips on the menus and navigation. This would also be a good news post to add a survey from Microsoft Forms, should people have questions. Alternatively, adding the relevant Yammer community on the News page and opening for discussions could be a great idea!

Closing

Viva Connections has my vote. The company Intranet has always been a priority of mine and the ability we have now to bring it all together in Microsoft Teams will have a positive impact on the adoption of the Intranet and consumption of corporate news.

PART IV

Microsoft Viva Topics

Microsoft Viva Topics is an organic way to provide employees access to knowledge and context around terms, content, and people within an organization. Viva Topics will engage employees by being surfaced in the applications they use every day such Microsoft Word, SharePoint, Teams, and Search within Microsoft 365.

CHAPTER 11

Introduction to Viva Topics

Before we dive into learning about Viva Topics, let's imagine a few business scenarios that you may encounter in your organization. Imagine a new-hire employee in a global company. She has joined a hybrid team within the IT Department as a UI/UX Developer. Part of her duties are to design and develop experiences that affect the entire organization. She needs to understand past projects that have taken place, find stakeholders to provide insight and business outcomes, and find the technologies and applications available to her. Specific acronyms have been mentioned in meetings and she continues to ask colleagues what they mean and some stakeholders reference past projects as inspiration for the new project she is working on. We will talk about how Viva Topics can help set her up for success and give her a glimpse into the history of other projects and the people who worked on them to help her prepare.

Next, let's consider a second scenario. You have a loyal employee from the Sales department. Over the past twenty years, he has managed some of the company's largest and most valued clients. Without a thought, he can tell you what products they order consistently, who are the primary stakeholders and contacts for the clients, and how the relationships with these clients have changed over the years. He is now looking to retire from the company and wants to ensure that the person who is taking over the accounts will avoid many of the hard-earned lessons that he encountered as a young account executive when he first started at the company. By helping his replacement understand the nuances of the region, what regulatory practices must be followed for each client, and cultural best practices, he will ensure the best possible outcomes as he embarks on his retirement.

A final scenario is an executive at the company who is in charge of forecasting a pipeline around a series of products that the company takes to market. He often needs to find financial data related to projects, products, and the resourcing needed to take those products to market. He creates presentations that combine terms, imagery, and data that comes from many other documents and data sources. He talks to managers and team members to gain insight about how products are currently selling in the market. He tries to search the corporate intranet to find information related to a specific product. These tasks take a lot of time away from his role as an executive in the company and rely on individual people within the organization to provide information.

Viva Topics will help the members of our scenarios to find information more easily from content that has been created within the organization. From the discovery of documents that may contain sales data to drive content for the executive to tell his story to the board to helping our UI/UX developer find information related to specific terms and acronyms to enable her to get up to speed on past projects quicker; each member of your organization will be able to leverage the power of Viva Topics to gain insights, historical knowledge, and enable productivity.

Viva Topics is powered through the use of artificial intelligence and with curated content from knowledge managers or content contributors within an organization. Viva Topics uses existing knowledge within the organization along with AI to create Topics Cards that can be used within the organization to help people discover terms, projects, events, products, locations, and much more that is just a click away.

We will dig into the details in the following chapters, but there are some things you should know before you get started with using Viva Topics. Viva Topics will provide the most value for medium to enterprise-sized companies as there is traditionally a larger range of content and knowledge across the organization. Smaller companies can introduce Viva Topics to help ensure that knowledge becomes available as the company continues to scale to get a head start.

Recommended Prerequisite Knowledge

As with any new skill or technology, you need the right people in the right roles to make a project successful. Being able to do a successful roll-out of Viva Topics within your organization is dependent upon having a strong team with knowledge in several areas such as people, processes, content, and strategy. We will talk more about people and the types of roles and responsibilities a little later. We will cover processes, content, and strategy when we talk about knowledge management

SharePoint

Viva Topics surface in many of the applications found within Microsoft 365. One of the primary applications is SharePoint. From within SharePoint, Viva Topics can be found and highlighted on SharePoint pages, news, and even search. The following SharePoint skills are desirable in order to configure and work with Viva Topics:

- How to create and edit site pages

- How to configure and work with Search scopes

- How to configure SharePoint permissions

- How to configure and apply sensitivity labels

- How to assign licenses to users

Teams

Let's take a moment and think about work and collaboration that are taking place in your organization. Team members are often working in Microsoft Teams to share conversations about projects and collaborate around topics and work product. In cases like these, you will want to ensure that no matter whether your team members are working in SharePoint or Teams, they will have a consistent experience and have access to content. Your team members should not have to think about what application to use to get information but be able to have a singular window to information regardless of the application in Office 365 as seen in Figure 11-1.

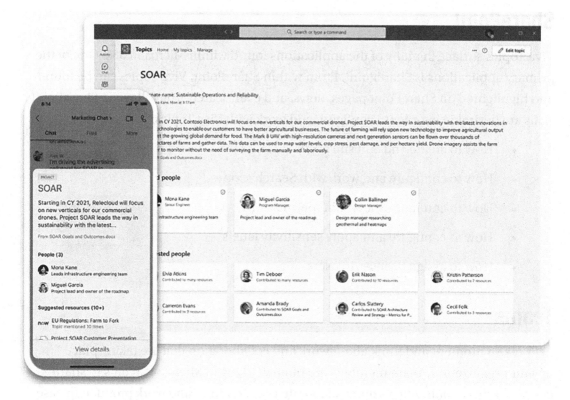

Figure 11-1. *Viva Topics in Microsoft Teams*

As a team member, you will be able to see topics being highlighted within posts inside of your Teams to identify additional information about a topic. When you hover over the highlighted topic, the topic card will show more information about the topic just as if you were looking at the topic card from within SharePoint as seen in Figure 11-2.

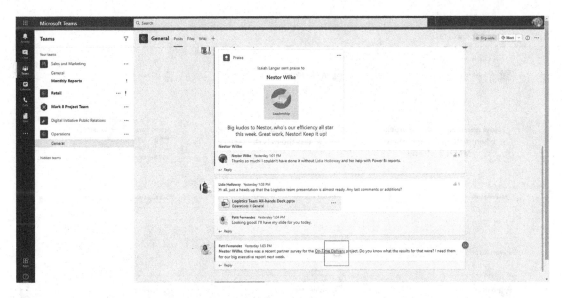

Figure 11-2. *Viva Topics in Microsoft Teams post*

If you would like Viva Topics to be surfaced within Teams, you will need to install and configure Viva Connections. In order to install, you will be required to install using the Viva Connections PowerShell Script.

Access the script: `https://bit.ly/2WaeOhD`

Yammer

Microsoft will be integrating several features from Yammer into Viva Topics. The first integration will focus on bringing the QnA features from within Yammer to be included on Viva Topic pages as seen in Figure 11-3. Microsoft has introduced Yammer into the Microsoft Viva ecosystem through Viva Engage. We will talk about Viva Engage through our additional resources section later in this book.

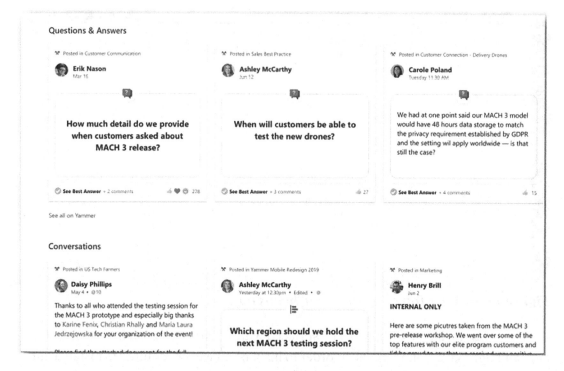

Figure 11-3. *Yammer QnA within a Viva Topic page*

You will also be able to view the same topic cards and topic highlighting experience that you already see through SharePoint and Microsoft Teams. In order to use Viva Topics effectively with the integration in Yammer, it will be important for you to provide change management and decision around what is a topic vs. what is a hashtag within Yammer post.

When you create a new post in Yammer and use a hashtag such as "#SalesGoals", the hashtag views as a link for you. When you click on that link, it will open search with a query for all messages that have been tagged with the hashtag "#SalesGoals". Previously, you could tag a Yammer post with a topic using the hashtag. This change will help prevent confusion and ensure that the experience for topics across your organization is consistent. When a post is tagged with a topic, a topic will show as a highlighted button below the primary content in the post. When you click on that button, it will take you to the topic page for that topic as seen in Figure 11-4.

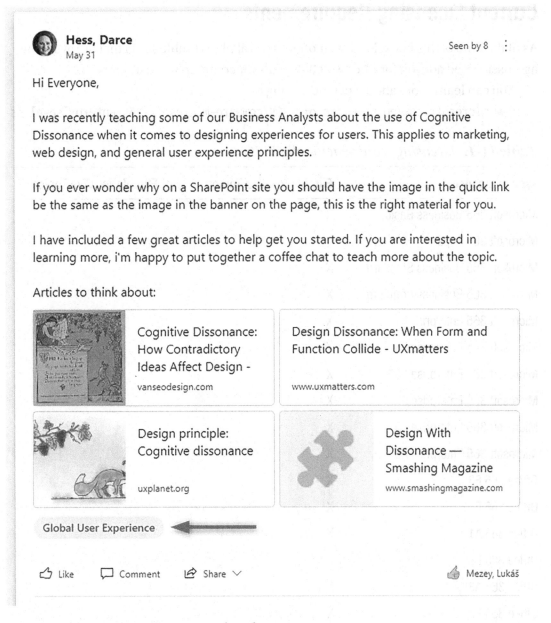

Figure 11-4. *Yammer post tagged with Viva Topic*

Ensuring that your users understand the difference on when to add a hashtag to a post or when to tag the post with a topic will ensure users have a seamless experience in their content discovery journeys.

Current Licensing Requirements

As of the time of this book, Microsoft offers several plans (Table 11-1) that are available as a user-based add-on for Microsoft 365 plans for commercial customers.

You can learn more about specific pricing at

www.microsoft.com/en-us/microsoft-365/compare-microsoft-365-enterprise-plans

Table 11-1. *Licensing requirements eligibility*

Type of License	Eligible for Viva Topics	Not Eligible for Viva Topics
Microsoft 365 Business Basic	X	
Microsoft 365 Apps		X
Microsoft 365 Business Standard	X	
Microsoft 365 Business Premium	X	
Microsoft 365 Enterprise F1	X	
Microsoft 365 Enterprise F3	X	
Microsoft 365 Enterprise E3	X	
Microsoft 365 Enterprise A3	X	
Microsoft 365 Enterprise E5	X	
Microsoft 365 Enterprise A5	X	
Office 365 F3	X	
Office 365 E1	X	
Office 365 A1	X	
Office 365 E3	X	
Office 365 A3	X	
Office 365 E5	X	
Office 365 A5	X	
SharePoint K Plan 1	X	
SharePoint K Plan 2	X	
Government Cloud* (potentially in second half of 2021)		X

Free Trial Information

You can receive a free trial that will provide you up to 25 licenses for 30 days. To qualify for a free trial, you must already have a qualifying Microsoft 365 or Office 365 plan. Since Viva Topics is reliant upon having a large set of data, including documents with different file types, SharePoint sites with pages, Microsoft Teams with posts and files, and potentially Yammer if used in your organization, it is recommended that you use a trial on your primary tenant that has content that can be consumed and leveraged by Viva Topics rather than trying Viva Topics on test tenants or tenants with little content or users. The larger the amount of the content and users, the more effective Viva Topics will be and the better the quality of the topics that will be identified.

Sign up for a free trial: `https://bit.ly/36PGFdF`

Summary

In this chapter, you gained a glimpse of the items and scenarios we will cover throughout Viva Topics. You learned about some basic knowledge that you and your teams will need to have to take advantage of Viva Topics and some basic licensing requirements.

CHAPTER 12

Configuring Viva Topics

Before taking the first steps to configuring Viva Topics within your tenant, it is important to understand what types of planning such as technical planning, including security, permissions management, licensing, and more that you should do ahead of time to be successful in your journey. The more planning that you do up front, the better chance you will have at a successful rollout and adoption of Viva Topics within your organization.

Technical Planning

Technical planning involves ensuring that you have the correct licensing in place to be able to use Viva Topics and other areas of Microsoft Viva within the applications you use every day. It will also involve making decisions regarding security and permissions management.

It is best when making decisions regarding the technical roll-out of Viva Topics to have a team be a part of the process. At the beginning, this should include someone from IT, someone from Legal to help determine if there are specific topics that should or should not be included, a member from Records Management or Knowledge Management, depending on the size of your organization. Records Management team members tend to have a high-level of experience with how documents and items are stored within the organization, the types of metadata that should be associated with them, and how those guidelines drive standardization within the organization.

Licensing

There are three available layers to licensing that you can choose. The first is having your Microsoft 365 license in place. Without any additional licensing, you would have access to use Microsoft Viva Connections and partial use of Viva Learning and Viva Insights. In order to assign a license, you must be Microsoft 365 administrator.

113

© D'arce Hess, Albert-Jan Schot, Tracy van der Schyff 2023
D. Hess et al., *Getting Started with Microsoft Viva*, https://doi.org/10.1007/978-1-4842-8590-9_12

The base Microsoft 365 licensing **does not** include support for Viva Topics. **All users** who will view, access, or curate topic pages and cards require the Viva Topics license.

There are two add-on options that will give you support for Viva Topics that we will talk about later. The Viva Topics Add-On and the additional Viva Suite. We will review the benefits and potential costs associated with each option and why you may want to include them in your Viva experiences.

Viva Topics Add-On

The Viva Topics Add-On is an annual subscription that is paid on a per-user basis. The Viva Topics add-on will enable your users to start to utilize Viva Topics without the additional items included in the larger Viva Suite. Viva Topics as an add-on will enable you to have the featured listed as follows.

What does it come with?

The Viva Topics Add-On provides the following additional services related to Viva Topics:

- Topic Cards, pages, and centers

- Topic Highlights in SharePoint, Office, and Microsoft Search

- Topic Highlights in Microsoft Teams. Outlook, and Yammer (coming in 2022)

- Answer concierge and contextual search (coming in 2022)

Why choose the Viva Topics Add-on?

If you are looking to get your feet wet with Microsoft Viva, Viva Topics is a great place to start. With the ability to quickly bring topics and knowledge identified through your workshops, you can drive the discoverability of information, resources, documentation, and people that are related to a specific topic. If we talk about the new employee scenario from earlier, she will be able to use Viva Topics to find template and mock-ups related to past projects and who the related UI/UX designers were on those projects to gain insights and develop extended relationships.

Where can I purchase the Viva Topics Add-On?

The Viva Topics Add-On is currently priced at $4.00 per user per month. If you have an enterprise-level organization, you may want to start with licensing for a subset of users such as your internal champions network. Starting off with a trial will allow you to work with your users and content managers to determine what the right topics are for consideration and create a small pilot of Viva Topics within your organization. This trial period will allow you to gather feedback from the subset of users to find the areas where Viva Topics will be the most useful such as with HR terminology and Benefits first or moving on to broader scenarios such as the content living within a help or QnA site. Once you work through your trial period internally, you can continue to add new users and licenses to organically grow topics adoption in alignment with your change management strategy.

To purchase the Viva Topics Add-On, visit: `https://bit.ly/3QX3JN5`.

You can gain access to a set of 50 licenses using the trial.

Microsoft Viva Suite

The Microsoft Viva Suite brings the entire suite of solutions including Viva Topics, Viva Learning, and Viva Insights. This suite is available through an annual subscription for $9.00 per-user per-month basis. You will learn more about what each vertical offers in the chapters to come.

Why choose the Viva Suite?

The Viva Suite will allow you to bring all of the Viva Experiences together. You can use topics to guide users toward information related to terms and topics within your org. You will add in insights to gain information about how your teams work and individual habits to drive balance and analytics and use Viva Learning to drive training and your learning experience from a unified solution.

Where can I purchase the Viva Suite Add-On?

The only option that currently provides a trial capability is Viva Topics. To engage with the other items in the suite, you will need to purchase licenses for the full suite.

To purchase the Microsoft Viva Suite subscription, visit: `https://bit.ly/3QShexA`

How to Apply Licenses

1. Within the Microsoft 365 Admin Center, select **Active Users** from the left navigation and select the user that you would like to add a license to.

2. Click the (…) to the right of the user's name and select **Manage product licenses** as shown in Figure 12-1.

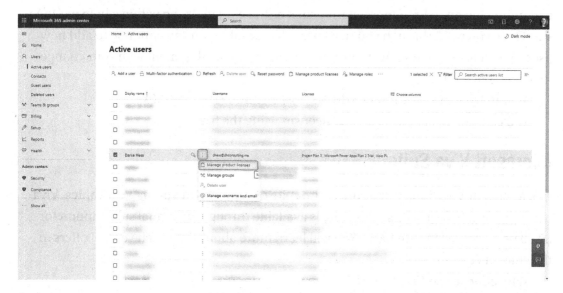

Figure 12-1. *Manage product licenses in Admin center*

3. Check the box for **Microsoft Viva Topics** and click the button to save changes as shown in Figure 12-2.

---

*It can take up to an hour for a user to get access to Topics after the license has been assigned.

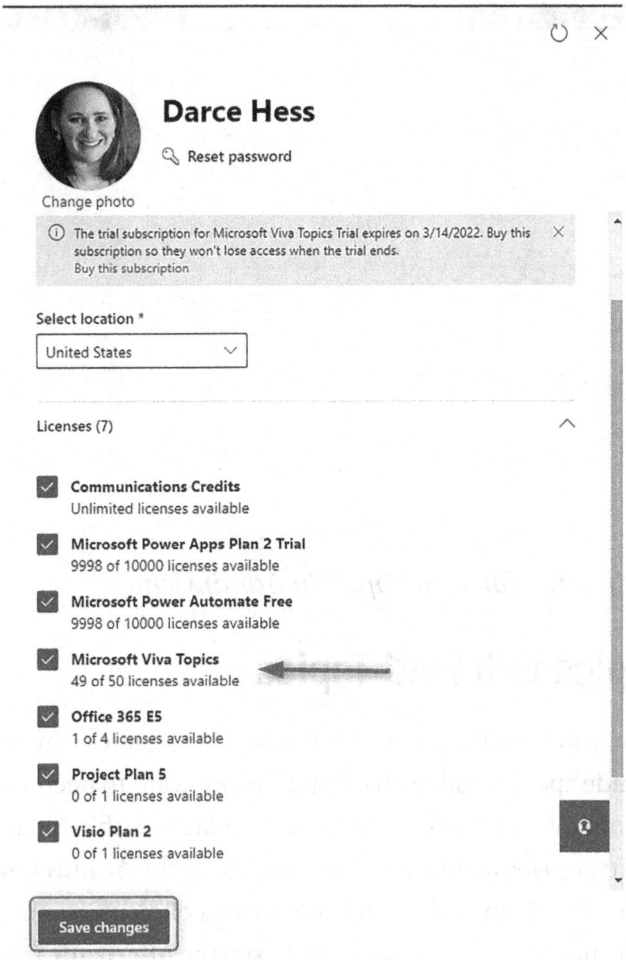

Figure 12-2. *Assign license to individual user*

Configure Viva Topics

Even though a user may have an assigned license within the tenant, you must first enable Topics to be discovered and curated by first setting up Viva Topics through the Admin Center. During the set-up process, you will determine who will be able to edit and view topics and where users will be able to see them.

To set-up Viva Topics, first navigate to the **Admin Center** and then to the **Setup** tab within the left navigation. Scroll to the bottom of the page under **Files and content** and select the radio button for **Connect people to knowledge with Viva Topics** as shown in Figure 12-3.

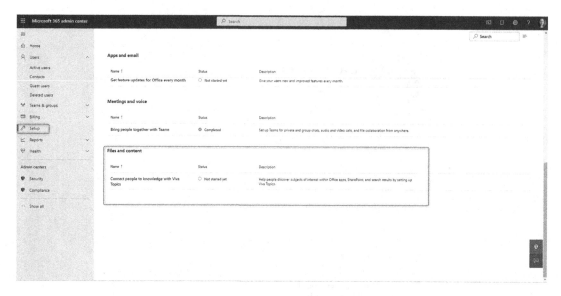

Figure 12-3. *Begin setup for Viva Topics in AdminCenter*

How Viva Topics Will Find Topics

As an administrator, you have the power to choose where topics can be crawled from as well as how to exclude specific topics that you may not want to become discoverable. Let's step back a moment and think about all of the places within SharePoint a Topic could be crawled. To adjust the settings, first navigate to the **Admin Center** and select the **Setup** and then select **Microsoft Viva** from the box choices. Depending on your screen size, you may need to scroll to the right to see the **Microsoft Viva** box appear as shown in Figure 12-4.

Figure 12-4. *Begin setup for Viva Topics in Admin Center*

Then select the choice **Connect people to knowledge with Viva Topics**
as shown in Figure 12-5.

Name ↑	Status	Description
Accelerate skilling and growth with Viva Learning		With Viva Learning, employees can easily discover and share everything from training courses to microlearning content.
Connect people to knowledge with Viva Topics	⊘ Completed	Help people discover subjects of interest within Office apps, SharePoint, and search results by setting up Viva Topics.
Inform, engage, and empower with Viva Connections		Viva Connections for Teams desktop combines the power of your intelligent SharePoint intranet with chat and collaboration tools in Microsoft Teams, making it easier than ever to reach and engage employees, bolster communication and connections, and empower people to succeed.

Figure 12-5. *Begin setup for Viva Topics in Admin Center*

You can then select **Manage** to view the panel with your options to edit the sources,
whether to exclude topics and much more as shown in Figure 12-6.

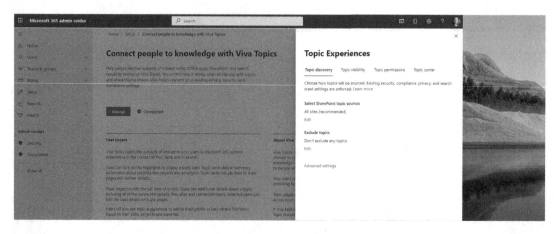

Figure 12-6. *Begin setup for Viva Topics in Admin Center*

1. **All Sites** – This is the recommended approach by Microsoft as it gives the widest net to being able to discover topics that user may want to learn about. With great power comes great responsibility as this type of crawl will not only crawl your intranet communication sites, but it will also crawl team sites that are standalone as well as Teams-connected team sites for Topics.

   Don't worry, all Topics are security-trimmed, meaning that all settings you have regarding permissions, security, and compliance also apply to Topics. Just like with search, a user will not be able to view a topic that they would not have permission to see.

2. **All, except selected sites** – Allows you to select which sites you want to crawl topics from. For example, if you only want to crawl for Topics that would live within your corporate intranet, but want to make sure that it does not crawl that one super-secret executives-only site as seen in Figure 12-7.

   This option is best if you only want to omit a few sites from your tenant. It is not recommended to use this option if you wanted to exclude all team sites, as an example, from your tenant.

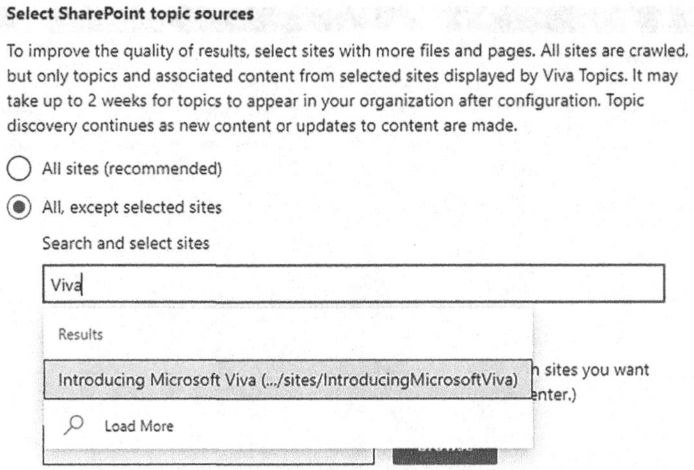

Select SharePoint topic sources

To improve the quality of results, select sites with more files and pages. All sites are crawled, but only topics and associated content from selected sites displayed by Viva Topics. It may take up to 2 weeks for topics to appear in your organization after configuration. Topic discovery continues as new content or updates to content are made.

◯ All sites (recommended)

⦿ All, except selected sites

Search and select sites

Viva

Results

Introducing Microsoft Viva (.../sites/IntroducingMicrosoftViva)   h sites you want
                                                                    enter.)

🔍   Load More

Figure 12-7. *Selecting specific SharePoint Sites for Topics*

If you have more than a handful of sites that you want to exclude, you can upload an Excel file with the list of sites that you want to include.

To get a complete list of all sites in your tenant as seen in Figure 12-8:

- navigate to the **SharePoint Admin Center**

- select **Active Sites** from the left navigation

- select **Export** at the top of the page to export a .csv file of all sites within your tenant

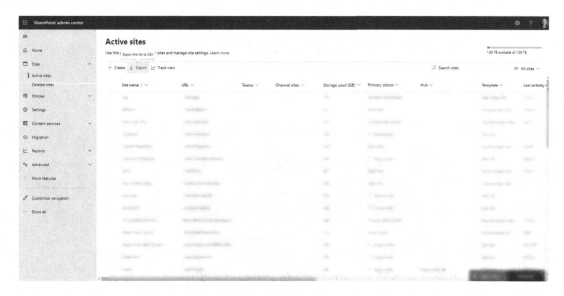

Figure 12-8. *Active Sites in SharePoint Admin Center*

3. **Only selected sites** – This option is best if you have more than a few sites that you want to allow to be crawled for Topics. If you have a corporate intranet with Communication Sites, and you only want to have the comms sites be crawled and exclude all the Team Sites within your organization, then this option is the right one for you.

    You can select specific sites to add, but like the option before, you can upload a .csv file containing all the sites that you would like to add vs. adding them individually through the interface.

4. **No Sites** – This option effectively removes the AI-driven discovery, curation, and updates for Viva Topics. It will still allow for manually curated Topics to be discovered by users within the organization, but all Topics would need to be manually created and maintained through the Topic Center.

Excluding Topics

In many organizations, there may be topics that you do not want to be discovered by users. These topics are often sensitive in nature such as workforce reduction plans.

You have two options:

1. **Don't exclude any topics** – This option will ensure that all potential topics can be crawled and will become available within the Topic Center, Topics Pages, and Topic Cards.

2. **Exclude topics by name** – This option provides you the ability to specifically exclude Topics by name. It can exclude the topics by full or partial name. If you have a lot of topics that you want to exclude, it would be best to use the .csv template that is available for download in the admin center to create a list of items that you do not want to be included.

To exclude a topic by name using the template, there are a few fields that you should gather:

- **Name** – This can be the exact name of the topic such as "DH Consulting", or you can do a partial match which could exclude all topics that have "DH" within the name. It will still allow for topics where dh may appear as part of the word such as "cardholders".

- **Stands for** (Optional) – Many organizations use acronyms to relay messaging or relationships of content. To exclude an acronym such as NDA, add the additional words as Non-Disclosure Agreement under the **Expansion** column within the template.

- **MatchType-Exact/Partial** – This will designate if the name that you have typed in is an exact match or a partial match.

You can also choose to **Exclude people from being suggested for Topics by AI** by navigating the **Topic Discovery** page and selecting the link for **Advanced Settings** as seen in Figure 12-9.

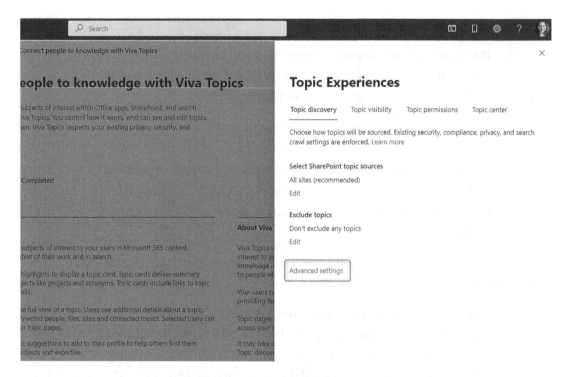

Figure 12-9. *Advanced settings in Topic Discovery page*

Choose Who Can See Topics

To select your options, you will first need to navigate to the **Topic Visibility** tab in the **Admin Center** as seen in Figure 12-10.

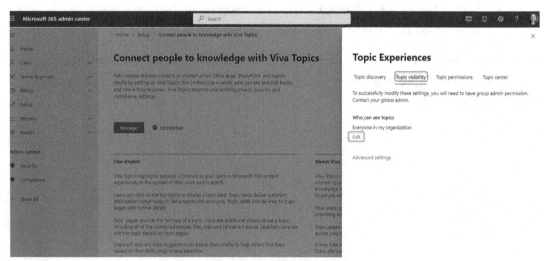

Figure 12-10. *Active Sites in SharePoint Admin Center*

There are three options to select from when it comes to determining who will be able to see topics within your organization. This choice may change over time. For example, while you and members of the knowledge management team are curating new topics within the Topic Center, you may not want to make Topics available to everyone in the organization at that time. You may choose to limit who can see the topics initially by a smaller pilot group based on a department or function to help gain feedback and test change management strategies. This time may also be taken to figure out frequently asked questions that can be transformed into a help page in your intranet.

The options are:

1. **Everyone in my organization** – This option includes everyone that has been given a Viva Topics license within the organization.

2. **Only selected people or security groups** – This is the perfect option to get you started when you are learning about Microsoft Viva Topics and starting to test with your pilot group. You can choose select individuals or you can use a pre-established Azure Active Directory Security Group. If you are planning on a large number of people starting for your pilot, you should consider using the AD Security Group rather than adding individual people.

3. **No one** – This will allow only the tenant administrator the ability to see anything that is related to topics. In a smaller organization where the administrator is providing multiple roles, this can be a good first step to learn and then branch out to the rest of the organization.

You may also select if **AI suggested topics are visible to users**. To adjust these settings for **All suggested topics –** or **No suggested topics**, select the **Advanced settings** link within the **Topic Visibility** page as seen in Figure 12-11.

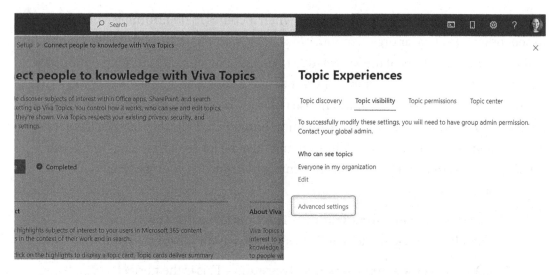

Figure 12-11. *Topic Visibility Advanced settings*

Control if AI suggested topics are visible to users as seen in Figure 12-12.

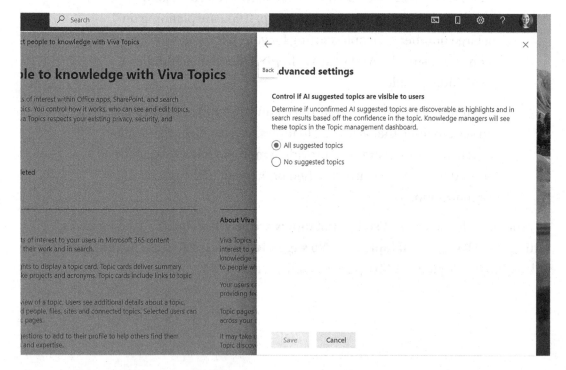

Figure 12-12. *Control if AI suggested topics are visible to users*

Setting Viva Topics Permissions

There are two important roles when it comes to permissions for topic management. You will need to make two decisions, who will be able to create and edit topics and who will be able to manage topics. Let's dive a little deeper into the difference between the two.

Before you can begin, you will need to navigate to the **Topic Permissions** page within the **Admin Center** as seen in Figure 12-13.

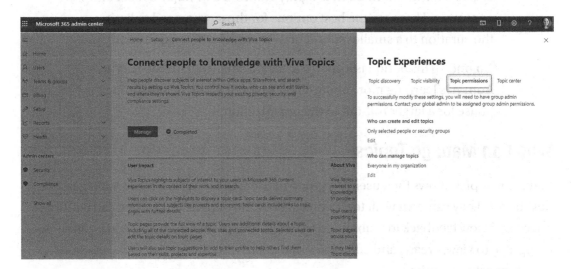

Figure 12-13. *Topic permissions in Admin Center*

Who Can Create and Edit Topics

As a topic is displayed from a topic card and into the topic page, any person who has access to edit can edit the content that lives within the topic page. They can update a description of a topic, the people that were identified as related to the topic by being a contributor of content containing references to that topic. Users who have permissions to this area do not have access to perform actions within the Topic management dashboard or review, confirm, or reject any topics. In this area, it can be beneficial to allow everyone in the organization to create and edit smaller details of a topic. By allowing everyone, you have a wider reach of people who know the content within the organization that can be valuable to others. The whole goal is to be able to identify content within the organization and help users discover those who contain the knowledge on that topic.

There are three options for configuring this area:

1. **Everyone in my organization** – Allows everyone who has a Microsoft Viva Topic license to create and edit topic pages.

2. **Only selected people or security groups** – The best option to choose if you want to maintain a tighter control over who can contribute to the curation and maintenance of topics. In some organizations, information is tightly controlled or requires specific approvals. These are the best options for those who need to limit the curation to a smaller subset of users within the organization.

3. **No one** – This option is a good starter if a single person such as an Admin is learning more about Viva Topics or is still in a planning phase for a larger roll-out to the organization.

Who Can Manage Topics

Managing topics allows for a user or a group of users to access the Topic management dashboard. They can review all topics throughout the organization. They can confirm, reject, and view feedback for submitted topics. These permissions come in addition to being able to view, create, and edit topics that come with the first set of permissions.

There are two options:

1. **Everyone in my organization** – This option would give full permissions to every person who has been assigned a Viva Topics license within the organization. For smaller organizations, this may be a good option as it gives everyone the opportunity to contribute toward the global knowledge management within the organization. Many larger companies prefer to have a more guided approach which would have them choose the next option.

2. **Only selected people or security groups** – This is the best option for larger enterprise organizations. It allows for a true governance setting of topics within the organization. It gives the opportunity for a select number of users or a group of users to manage the overall topics within the organization and can also see feedback and create a workflow process around implementing feedback on topics.

Create a Topic Center

The Topic Center is a SharePoint Site Collection. Each topic that is created will live as a site page within this site collection. This will become the centralized location for knowledge managers to curate new topic pages and manage topics.

The name of the topic center should be something easy for users to recognize within the organization. Using a name such as "Topics" will help with adoption as users can relate Viva Topics to the name "topics" in a URL.

To begin, navigate to the **Admin Center** and select the **Topic Center** page as seen in Figure 12-14.

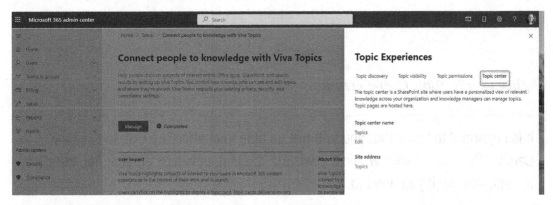

Figure 12-14. *Topic center page in Admin Center*

Set up your topic center by

1. Adding a topic center name in the **site name** field.

2. Providing a different URL address if you need to.

3. Providing a new description or keeping the default description for the site collection.

4. Clicking **Next** to continue as seen in Figure 12-15.

Figure 12-15. *Topic Center creation*

It is important to know that you **will not** be able to change the URL to the Topic
Center after you activate within the wizard. You can, however, change the name of
the site later on if you need to.

After activation, you will receive a confirmation page confirming all of your
selections during the setup process as seen in Figure 12-16.

Figure 12-16. *Viva Topic configuration complete confirmation*

If you ever need to change any of your preferences, you can return to the setup wizard by navigating to the **Microsoft 365 Admin Center**. Select **Setup** from the left-navigation and then select **Microsoft Viva** on the right and finally, select **Manage** as seen in Figure 12-17. You will likely adjust these settings as you explore a full roll out of Viva Topics expanding out from your initial pilot groups.

Figure 12-17. Manage Viva Topics settings in Admin Center

It can take up to two weeks for topics to appear in your organization after you have finished configuration.

Summary

In this chapter, we covered what content should be considered when implementing technical planning and who should be involved in the decision-making process for implementing Viva Topics. We talked about what licensing is available through the Viva Topics Add-On and the Viva Suite, how to get started, and where to purchase licenses or try the Viva Topics experience through a trial. You learned how to add people to the different management groups to allow the creation and editing of topics in your environment. You also learned how to provision your Topic Center, configure the visibility and governance capabilities for Viva Topics within SharePoint. In the next chapter, we will cover how Viva Topics can be integrated into your knowledge management guiding principles.

CHAPTER 13

Topics' Role in Knowledge Management

In order to bring knowledge to the organization using Viva Topics, you need to understand what types of knowledge you are working with and the best way to cultivate and discover them within an organization. We will explore the different types of knowledge shown in Figure 13-1. These concepts exist no matter the size of the organization.

To have a successful roll out and adoption of Viva Topics, having a solid understanding of knowledge management is key. Don't worry if you aren't the expert in your organization. In many enterprise organizations, you will find the experts hidden away in records management, librarians, and information architects.

In this chapter, we will learn about Knowledge Management in the context of maximizing your success and getting the most out of Viva Topics. The concepts we will cover exist in all organizations, regardless of the size of the organization. And don't worry if you aren't the expert. In many enterprise organizations, employees in those roles tend to be confined to positions like records management, librarians, or information architects.

What Is Knowledge Management?

It's always good to start with a little history to understand how we have evolved to where we are now. A definition of Knowledge Management by the Garter Group states

> *Knowledge management is a discipline that promotes an integrated approach to identifying, capturing, evaluating, retrieving, and sharing all of an enterprise's information assets. These assets may include databases, documents, policies, procedures, and previously un-captured expertise and experience in individual workers.*

Sounds easy, right?

D. Hess et al., *Getting Started with Microsoft Viva*, https://doi.org/10.1007/978-1-4842-8590-9_13

Types of Knowledge

There are three common types of knowledge: Tacit, Explicit, and Implicit knowledge. All types of knowledge are valuable. Let's dive a little deeper to get a better understanding of each of these types of knowledge and where you may encounter them within your organization.

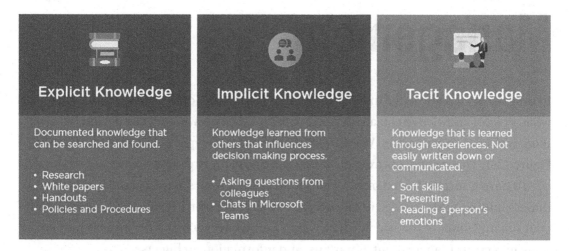

Figure 13-1. *Types of Knowledge*

Explicit Knowledge

Explicit knowledge is all the written and accessible knowledge that we have access to. Explicit knowledge is easily articulated to others. It can be recorded, documented, and most importantly, stored, and referenced within an organization. An example of explicit knowledge within an organization can be white papers, research, reports, and pages within your intranet.

Implicit Knowledge

Implicit knowledge is the application of explicit knowledge. Have you ever had to ask someone in the organization how to do a task? There may be several options on how to perform that task that are not documented, but all are valid. The knowledge that is gained from the person asked is implicit knowledge. It is not written down, but it has been learned through trial and error or word-of-mouth. The skills that are gained through these experiences is implicit knowledge. When a colleague shares information through a post within Microsoft Teams to share their knowledge, they are sharing implicit knowledge that you and others can learn from.

Tacit Knowledge

Tacit knowledge is the knowledge that each of us have learned from personal experiences. This is the knowledge that if someone asked us, it would be difficult to write down, articulate, or provide back to someone else. An example of tacit knowledge may be how to be a leader. While someone can take a class to gain a specific set of skills, there is often a quality found in great leaders that isn't taught, it has been gained through their experiences and how those experiences shaped how they work with others in the future. Another example may be the quality of having emotional intelligence. The ability to read other's emotions to help influence an outcome is something that is often difficult to teach others.

In an organization, tacit knowledge is the application of implicit knowledge that is specific to your organization.

Where Does Viva Topics Fit In?

Viva Topics bring both Explicit and Implicit knowledge to life within your organization. Imagine the scenario we mentioned in the introduction. You have a member of the organization who is about to retire and leave the organization. Over the course of their decades-long career at your organization, they have gained both explicit knowledge of all the documented processes and details as well as Implicit knowledge and how to get things done. When that person leaves the organization, generally, all that historical knowledge leaves with them. One of the primary goals of Viva Topics is to help that person share all the knowledge that they have learned over the years so that others can also learn from their experiences and knowledge so that it does not leave the organization when a specific person leaves.

Microsoft Viva Topics uses AI to scan explicit knowledge throughout the services that you use every day such as your company intranet built on SharePoint or even your email from a colleague explaining how to create that new contract for a client. Within my own day, I discovered that I spent sometimes over 15 minutes trying to search my email for a message I got from a colleague or something that I had sent someone else that they are asking for once more. Those 15 minutes add up over the course of the week, month, and year and can cost a lot in productivity and actual cost in time for myself and the company or clients I provide services for. In Figure 13-2, we show three of the primary ways people share information within organizations.

Information is not always shared in a uniform or consumable way within an organization. For many organizations, email is still the primary tool for sharing information, while closely followed by corporate intranets and company meetings. Think about how much time you spend searching through emails to find that one piece of information about a project that was shared or where you last saw the explanation of the new acronym within the organization.

Figure 13-2. *Primary ways knowledge is shared within an organization*

Let's take some of that time spent in training and searching and get it back in-context and at the time we need it the most. That is our goal with Viva Topics.

Common Search Issues that Viva Topics Can Help With

Viva Topics will help to solve some of the common problems that we see in organizations such as:

- Knowing where to search for a specific item or content such as a term or a specific document

- Understanding that the way different people search or find content varies from person-to-person

- Knowing which search result is correct or what the source of truth is

- Content lives within different applications and provides a fractured experience for users looking to find content in a consumable way

By using Viva Topics, we can address the ability for a user to find that right term or related information on a Topic. This can become explicit knowledge and something that you will know by the representation of a Topic highlight within an email they received or in that latest PowerPoint presentation from another team. You can now, without asking someone, gain access to a whole world of knowledge that is curated for you in a way that will help you gain context, understanding, and know who to ask for help if you have additional questions.

People search in different ways. I have sat behind users and asked them to look for something and seen them take an approach I had never thought of. It is important that we help to deliver experiences that can help everyone. Since people search sometimes by scanning content for discovery and in other cases, looking for that one specific document you created, Viva Topics helps to identify those relationships between what you are looking and what you want to know by providing the Topics pages with additional content as well as the Topic Cards from the highlighted topic to give you context and inform that there is more information about the topic.

Viva Topics provides a source of truth for terms and content within the organization. In the past, you may have searched for a document to get ready for a presentation and found that there were four versions of it. You know you have all seen the example of "ThisDocumentName_Final_no_this_Is_the_final_I_promise" in your local SharePoint library. Viva Topics will help to identify the documents that are the most relevant based on the item you searched for to help prevent confusion and create that source of truth for information.

Another common scenario is that content and information live in different systems and applications. Some you may have access to and others you may not. Nothing is more frustrating when I was told to go to a certain folder or system to get information only to find out I didn't have the right permissions to access it. Viva Topics will search in your most common applications such as Outlook, SharePoint, Yammer, and Microsoft Teams to provide cues back to you no matter where that content lives, helping to provide a seamless experience for users and relieve some of that frustration.

Conclusion

In this chapter, you learned about explicit knowledge, tacit knowledge, and implicit knowledge. You learned how to identify them as well as how to think about knowledge within your organization. Everything from that brand new employee that is starting all the way through the long-time employee that is retiring and their journey on how they consume and contribute knowledge back to your users and organization over time. In the next chapter, we will talk about some of the roles and responsibilities needed to bring Viva Topics to life in your organization.

CHAPTER 14

Viva Topics' Roles and Responsibilities

Before you can create your first topic, you should become familiar with the roles and responsibilities in order to have a successful rollout of Viva Topics. While multiple roles may be covered by a single person, it is recommended to have different people fulfill each of the following roles to ensure multiple perspectives and organizational knowledge are considered. When considering people to fulfill these roles, be sure to consider people on the business side of the organization and not just those who are in IT. By partnering with members of the business, you will gain more insight into potential topics, business processes, and knowledge that should be discoverable by everyone in the organization.

Roles in Viva Topics

Administrators

As an Administrator, you control all of the settings for Viva Topics within the Microsoft 365 admin center. In order to fulfill this role, you must be a Microsoft 365 Admin or a SharePoint Admin. You are required to do the initial setup of the Topic Center and initial configuration of Viva Topics within the organization.

Knowing that technical admins may not always have their pulse on the information coming out of the business, you should partner with members of the business, including individuals from Legal, Records Management (Table 14-1), and the departments or functions, to have a better understanding of what information should be allowed to become topics and, more importantly, if there is any information or terms that should not be discoverable (Figure 14-1).

© D'arce Hess, Albert-Jan Schot, Tracy van der Schyff 2023
D. Hess et al., *Getting Started with Microsoft Viva*, https://doi.org/10.1007/978-1-4842-8590-9_14

Table 14-1. *Example business partners and associated skills*

Example Business Partner	Associated expertise that can contribute to Viva Topics
Legal Business Partner	• Identify types of contracts such as MSLA, Licensing, etc. • Legal terms and acronyms such as Non-Disclosure Agreement (NDA) • Identify templates or legal forms Identify items that should not become topics for legal or regulatory reasons such as content that may have PII information
Human Resources Business Partner	• Identify Policies and Procedures to become topics • Provide context around benefits information Provide information related to onboarding activities that can become topics
Sales Business Partner	• Client Information, including contacts, previous contracts, product orders • Regional information such as cultural references and acronyms Language-specific content if information is country-based
IT Business Partner	• Software and Application names and their use cases in the organization • Technology Acronyms such as CI/CD or SDLC • Help site content such as user guides and documentation Service or Application Owners

Areas That the Administrator Can Contribute To

- Select which SharePoint sites will be crawled for topics.

- Selecting which licensed users can view topics.

- Select with topics or terms that should be excluded from being topics.

- Select who can create or edit topics.

- Select who will be able to manage topics.

- Creation and naming of the Topic Center.

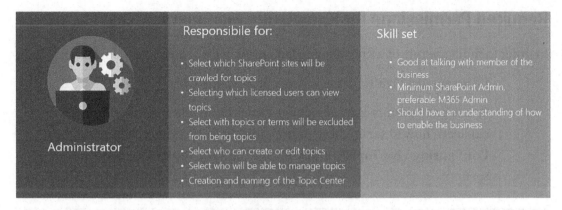

	Responsibile for:	Skill set
Administrator	• Select which SharePoint sites will be crawled for topics • Selecting which licensed users can view topics • Select with topics or terms will be excluded from being topics • Select who can create or edit topics • Select who will be able to manage topics • Creation and naming of the Topic Center	• Good at talking with member of the business • Minimum SharePoint Admin, preferable M365 Admin • Should have an understanding of how to enable the business

Figure 14-1. *Skills and responsibilities of the administrator*

Knowledge Manager

A knowledge manager is the person(s) who manage the topics for the organization within the Topic Center (Figure 14-2). Only the users identified as a knowledge manager will be able to view and edit topics from the **Manage Topics** section of the Topic Center.

A Knowledge Manager should have a good understanding of the business overall. This is often someone at a manager level and would be able to know if certain topics may be related to each other or determine if a topic is valid. For instance, could a topic about a custom dashboard also be associated to a topic regarding Power BI?

Areas That the Knowledge Manager Can Contribute To

- View AI-suggested topics.

- Review and confirm validity of AI-suggested topics.

- Remove topics that should not be visible to users.

- Create new topics.

- Edit existing topics.

Required Permissions for Knowledge Managers

In order to fulfill the role of a Knowledge Manager, you must have the following:

- Be assigned a Viva Topics license by an administrator.

- Be assigned permissions to manage topics by an administrator. You can learn how to set up these permissions in the previous chapter on **Configuring Viva Topics** under the **Setting Viva Topics Permissions** section.

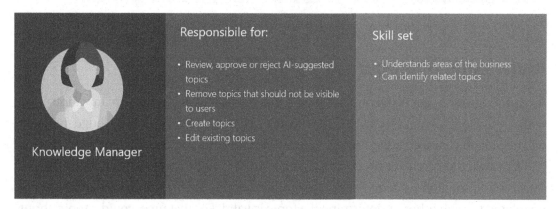

Figure 14-2. *Skills and responsibilities of a knowledge manager*

Topic Contributors

Topic Contributors are going to be your primary source of people who are curating the topics within the organization (Figure 14-3). They will be creating the content within the topic pages for both the manually curated as well as the AI-generated topics. These users can be pulled from someone who would traditionally be a business analyst or an administrative assistant. They should have good writing and communication skills and be ok with new technology that will continue to evolve.

Required Permissions for Topic Contributors

To be a Topic Contributor, you must have the following:

- Be assigned a Viva Topics license by an administrator.

- Be assigned permissions to create and edit topics through the admin center. You can learn how to set up these permissions in the previous chapter on **Configuring Viva Topics** under the **Setting Viva Topics Permissions** section.

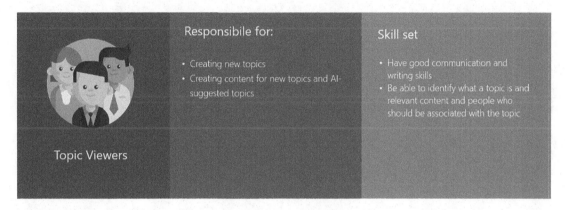

Figure 14-3. *Skills and responsibilities of the Topic viewers*

Summary

In this chapter, we reviewed the roles that can be assigned for Viva Topics within your organization. While each of these roles can be adapted to be filled by one or more people in the business, it is most important that you find the right people to provide insight into the types of content that will need to be discoverable by users and people with the ability to clearly communicate those topics through the associated topic pages in the topic center.

CHAPTER 15

Creating and Working with Topics and Topic Pages

Viva Topics can be created two different ways. Either by using AI or through manual creation by a user. In this chapter, we are going to learn how you can use the AI to your advantage to discover and suggest topics in cooperation with manual topics. Identifying these topics will become the key to growing adoption of Viva Topics within your organization.

AI-Suggested Topics

There are several areas within your organization that you may want to use as base topics for your organization. A primary example is with information related to IT. In many organizations, users often have a lack of understanding around common terminology, applications, products, or help resources. Let's take products as an example. Your company could produce fifty separate products. Each of these products has a team that is responsible for it, a series of related documentation, past and current projects, and perhaps specific terminology that is used around it. If a person in your organization learned that you make a specific product, how would they find information about it? Would they ask the person sitting next to them? Would they search the company intranet? If they did, would they get the right answers that you want them to know? They answer is "maybe." Very few people in an organization know everything about a specific product or project. If you select Topics as your source of truth, you can create a topic related to a product. That topic can help the user discover who are the official sources that worked on the projects, that past documentation that someone forgot to put in the right place, and information they hadn't even thought about such as related products or dependencies such as parts or other products. It can help to bridge the gaps between what people know and what they need to know. AI will also suggest topics based on

© D'arce Hess, Albert-Jan Schot, Tracy van der Schyff 2023
D. Hess et al., *Getting Started with Microsoft Viva*, https://doi.org/10.1007/978-1-4842-8590-9_15

topics you may have contributed resources to. For example, a topic may exist around Amazon Web Services. If you created or edited a page in SharePoint where AWS or Amazon Web Services was mentioned, AI is going to ask you if you want to be listed on that topic as someone who has produced content related to that topic. Remember that the outcome you are looking to achieve is helping users within your organization find information about a specific topic or term and the related information to it when they need it.

Types of AI-Suggested Topics

Microsoft AI will suggest topics based on a few types:

- Project

- Event

- Organization

- Location

- Product

- Creative work

- Field of study

When the AI finds a specific type of potential topic, it determines whether or not there is enough information for it to become a topic to the knowledge manager via the Topic Center (Figure 15-1). AI will also look for additional information related to the topic. Let's use our example of Amazon Web Services. AI will look for any alternative names or acronyms that the topic could be used as. In this case, Amazon Web Services may also be identified by the acronym "AWS." AI will identify a description of the topic such as "AWS" is the hosting and storage provider for all cloud-based applications for the IT Department. It will also identify people who might be knowledgeable about the topic by having authored content in SharePoint, Teams, or documents that contained the terms used. This means that Sam from IT was identified because his name was on a project document where AWS was mentioned as well as Sara from Finance because she signed the contracts to approve the use of AWS at the company. AI is also going to search through SharePoint sites, Microsoft Teams, and documents to discover items where AWS was also used. This will result in sites and documents also being recommended to users through the topic, as long as the user has the permissions to view that content in its location. This will help user discover the training communication site about AWS as well as any training documents, but they will not see the contract that Sara signed as it is located in a private Finance site where only the members of that site would see it.

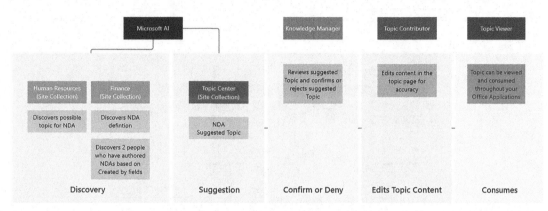

Figure 15-1. *Topics identification and process workflow*

AI-suggested Topics will not automatically be available to users. They must be reviewed and confirmed by Knowledge Managers in the Topic Center before they will become available to users. This is for several reasons. The first is security. AI could identify a potential topic called "Staff Reductions" because it showed up in documents and content that was being produced by senior executives at the company. While this may be a topic, it may not be appropriate for a larger audience. Another example may be the term "checklist." The term may be used to describe types of documents that exist, but the term itself may be too generic and not have a specific business purpose where it would warrant having its own topic page dedicated to it. By having a Knowledge Manager review and confirm the suggested topic, it will ensure that the topic AI suggestion is actually valid, meets the need of the business, and that the content and people identified as related are also correct or can be adjusted before being approved. Once the Knowledge Manager approves the topic, then it can be viewed by users.

Suggested Topics in Topic Center

Knowledge managers can view AI-suggested topics through the **Manage topics** tab (Figure 15-2) within the Topic Center.

Figure 15-2. *A view of the Manage Topics tab in the Topic Center*

In a larger organization, you could see that AI-suggested topics can reach into the thousands based on the information that is available from sources such as site collections. The graph will show the increase over time of how many suggested topics are being discovered within the organization. It helps to show you the progress that AI is making as more content is created within the organization.

There are several columns available that represent metadata that the AI has gathered that it has determined is associated with the Topic.

Quality Score

The Quality Score will show how much information that an average user will see regarding the topic. Some users may see more or less information regarding the topics depending on the specific permissions that they have to the direct content.

This Quality Score will help knowledge managers more easily determine which suggested topics may have more information relevant to the organization and confirm those topics first while reviewing other suggested topics.

Name

The Name of the topic is the suggested name based on the AI discovery.

Discovered

This date shows when AI initially discovered the topic within the organization. As your data and content continues to grow, you will see that AI will continue to crawl and discover new topics that may be relevant within your organization.

Impressions

The Impressions column will show how many times a topic has been shown to end users through topic answer cards in search and through topic highlights. Impressions are important as they help drive social interaction and increased engagement from users. The more times that a topic is seen, the higher the chance that a user will click on the topic and want to learn more.

Suggested People

Suggested people are aggregated from people who have written or edited documents that contain any kind of topic evidence for that topic. If one particular document that a person was the author of contains a lot of information about that topic, that person may become a suggested person (Figure 15-3); however, it is better to have multiple people suggested as it shows more evidence and a stronger connection to the topic if multiple people have contributed to the topic in the organization.

Figure 15-3. *Identifying suggested people*

When suggested people are shown, you will see how they are connected to the topic by the name and link to the document they contributed to that contained information about the topic or the SharePoint site they created or modified a page with information related to the topic.

Alternate Names

Alternate names are other names that a topic may be recognized by. This is very important when you are using acronyms within an organization. For example, an NDA may be the topic, but it also may be known or recognized as a "Non-Disclosure Agreement." Some topics may have multiple names associated with them. Some may be the actual formal identification, but departments or teams may call the topic a less formal name for identification.

Confirm a Suggested Topic

To confirm a suggested topic, navigate to the **Manage topics** tab within the Topic Center.

1. Hover to the right of the topic name. You will see a check mark and an X.

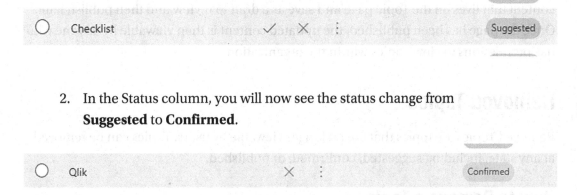

2. In the Status column, you will now see the status change from **Suggested** to **Confirmed**.

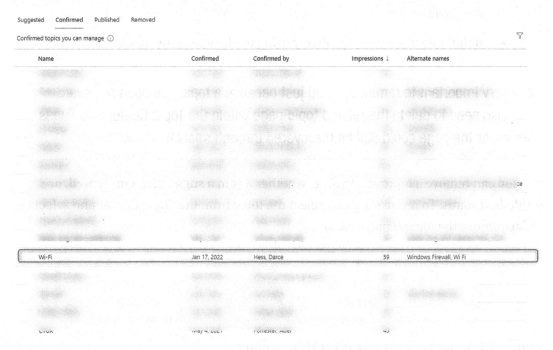

Once your topic has been confirmed (Figure 15-4), you will then see the topic show within the **Confirmed** tab. Topics can also be confirmed if the topic receives at least two positive votes through the feedback mechanism.

Figure 15-4. *The topic now appears listing in the "confirmed" tab*

Published Topics

Published Topics are topics that have been manually curated by a user. This includes topics in which manual edits have been made to improve the quality of the topic.

Since a topic page is a SharePoint Site Page, it maintains the publishing process the same as a regular SharePoint page. This will allow an editor to make a change to the content that lives on the Topic page and save as a draft to review and then publish later. Once the page has been published, the updated content is then viewable by anyone who has permissions to view Topics within the organization.

Removed Topics

Removed Topics are topics that are no longer viewable by users. Topics can be removed at any state, including suggested, confirmed, or published.

How to Remove a Topic

A topic can be removed through a couple ways:

- A Knowledge Manager removes the topic in the **Manage topics** tab in the Topic Center

- If multiple users vote negatively using the feedback mechanism.

It is very important to remember that just because a topic has been removed, you also need to delete the related topic page within the Topic Center Site Pages library, or the page could still be discovered through **search.**

You can remove a topic at any time, whether it is in a **suggested**, **confirmed**, or **published** status. To remove a topic, select the topic from the Topic Center and select the "**X**" to remove the topic (Figure 15-5).

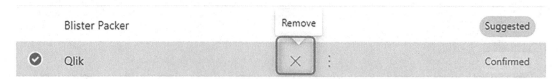

Figure 15-5. *Removing topic from Topic Center*

If the topic was published before you removed it, it can take up to 24 hours for the topic to stop appearing for users. This is because the topic is also indexed by search and will need to wait for the next indexing of content to ensure its removal from view. Since each topic gets an associated page in the Site Pages library of the Topic Center, you will need to delete the associated page separately within the Site Pages library in order to ensure the topic is completely removed from search (Figure 15-7).

Manually Curated Topics

Manually curated topics are topics that are created by a user within your organization. These are usually known content that should become available or distributed to users such as the name of a particular tool, resource, or acronym that has a very specific definition or subject matter expert.

Create a New Topic

1. To create a new topic, navigate to your Topic center and select **Topic Page** (Figure 15-6) from the **New** dropdown.

Figure 15-6. *Creating a Topic Page*

2. Complete the fields in the template (Figure 15-7) on the Topic Page:

   a. Name of Topic (Required)

   b. Alternate names (optional)

   c. Description (Required)

   d. Pinned People

   e. Pinned files and pages

   f. Pinned sites

   g. Related topics

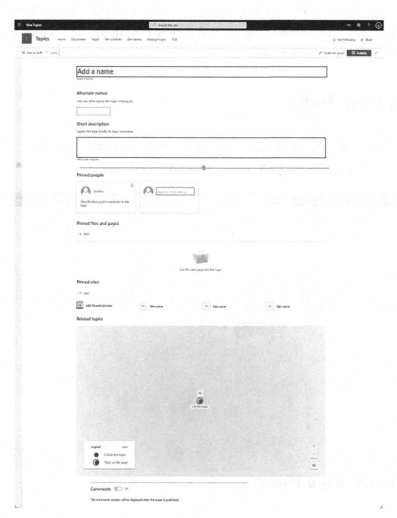

Figure 15-7. *Complete the fields*

3. Once you have completed the content on the page, click **Publish** to publish and make public the content within the page.

Remove a Topic Page

If you remove a topic from the topic center, you also need to remove the associated topic page.

1. To remove a topic page, go to the Topic center and access the **Site Pages** library from Site contents (Figure 15-8).

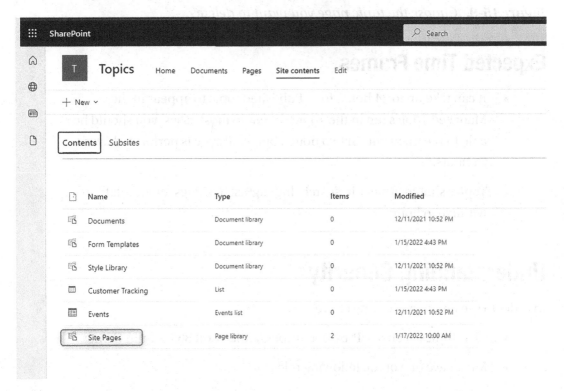

Figure 15-8. *Select the site pages library*

2. Select the topic page that you want to remove and select **Delete** from the menu as shown in Figure 15-9.

Figure 15-9. *Choose the topic page you want to delete*

Expected Time Frames

- It can take up to 24 hours for a Published topic to appear in the Managed Topics tab in the Topic center. In most cases, you should be able to see them within two hours, but a full sync is performed every 24 hours.

- Topics should appear in search, highlights, hashtags, or annotations within two hours

Understanding Security

In order to see topics, a user must have

- Viva Topics license – Provided through Microsoft 365 Admin Center.

- Must have one of the following roles:

  - Topic Viewer

  - Topic Contributor

  - Knowledge Manager

The three roles mentioned above provide the user with access to topics through the Topic Center and Topic Cards.

Viva Topics respects the permissions of the source content. This means that if a user does not have access to the source, they will not have access to the topic. This will prevent a user from accidentally discovering a topic that is sensitive or restricted.

What Parts of a Topic Are Seen by Users

Topic item	What a user can see
Topic name	Users can see the topic name of topics in the topic center. Some topics may not be visible if users don't have permissions to the source content or have a low relevancy to the user
Topic description	AI-generated descriptions are visible only to users who have permissions to the source content. Manually entered or edited descriptions are visible to all users.
People	Pinned people are visible to all users. Suggested people are only visible to users who have permissions to the source content.
Files	Files are only visible to users who have permissions to the source content.
Pages	Pages are only visible to users who have permissions to the source content.
Sites	Sites are only visible to users who have permissions to the source content.

What About Email or a User's OneDrive?

Topics are discovered through specified SharePoint sites that are determined during the setup of Viva Topics and can be changed through the Admin Center. You can find out more about setting up which site are Topics sources in the **Configuring Viva Topics** chapter in the **How Viva Topics will find Topics** section. Viva Topics will not discover items that live within a user's email or their OneDrive.

Guests and External Users

To allow guest users to view Topics, they will need to be granted a license. In this case, you will want to add them by selecting **"Only Selected people or security groups"** from the options during the initial configuration of Topics. All users who will view Topics must be granted a license including Guest users.

Where Do Users See Topics

Topics can be seen by users in a few different locations:

- Highlighted on SharePoint Pages

- Search results

- Search in Office Applications

- Topic Center home page

- Yammer

- Microsoft Teams

- Microsoft Outlook

SharePoint Highlights

When a user places content on a SharePoint page using the Text web part, the text within the web part on the page can reference topics (Figure 15-10). If a topic has been identified within the text, the topic will have a grey background designating it as a topic in the Topic Center.

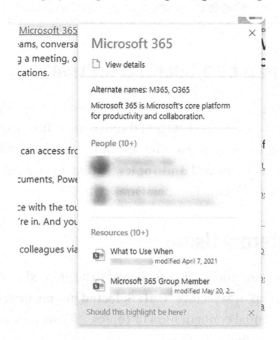

Figure 15-10. *Referencing Topics*

The user can hover over the topic name to bring up the topic card where they can view additional details about the topic such as the alternate names, description, people related to the topic and resources.

Topic Highlights bridge the knowledge gap by providing users access to knowledge within the context of where they are at that moment.

Search Results

When you search from the SharePoint start page, a SharePoint Site Collection, or the Office.com page for an item, a topic answer will appear (Figure 15-11) at the top of the search results and share the same information that is available through the topic card.

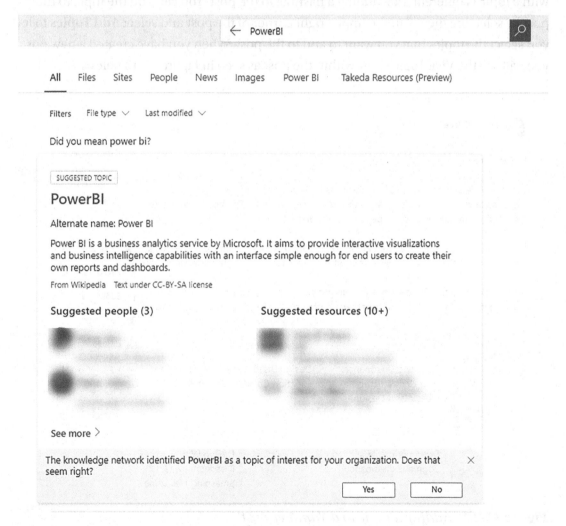

Figure 15-11. *View of a topic description*

Office Application Search

Office applications include Outlook, Excel, Word, etc., when a user is within a document and performs a search.

The results will appear within a right panel (Figure 15-12). This allows you to discover a possible topic in the context of looking for more information without having to go into a separate search center.

Yammer

Yammer posts can be tagged with a Viva Topic. It is important to note that tagging a post with a topic is different than adding a hashtag to the post. You can add the topic to the post by selecting the "..." in the upper-right corner of the post and select **Add Topics** to let you select the topics that you want to add to the post. When you have created a new post, you will see the Viva Topic show within the post as seen in Figure 15-13 below.

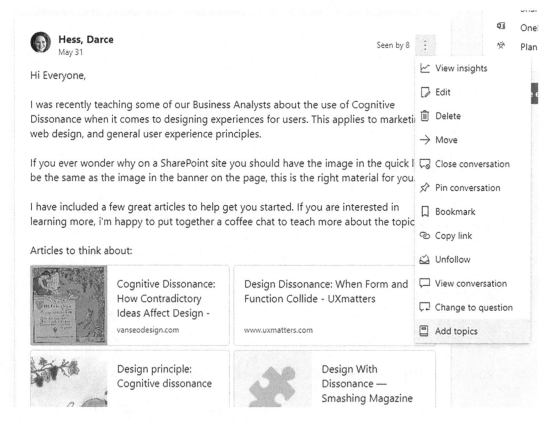

Figure 15-12. *Adding a topic to a Yammer post*

You can select more than one topic. If the topic does not already exist, Viva Topics will ask you if you want to create the topic. Until you create the topic, you will not be able to tag the post.

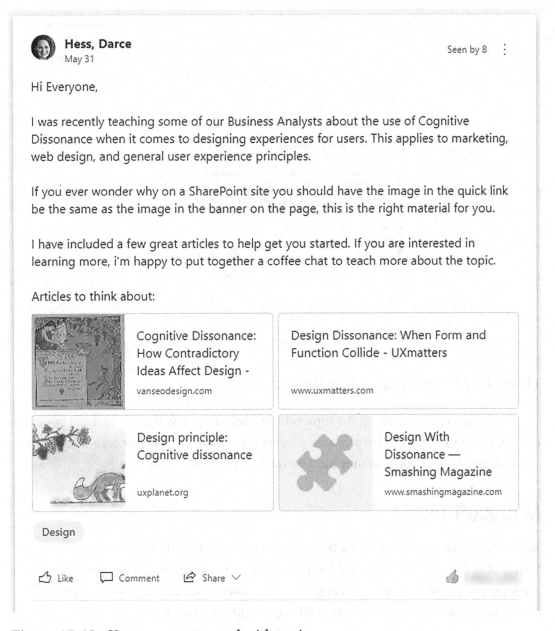

Figure 15-13. Yammer post tagged with topic

When you click on the topic from the Yammer post, you will view the topic page within Yammer and see other posts that have also been tagged with that topic within the Yammer interface as shown in Figure 15-14.

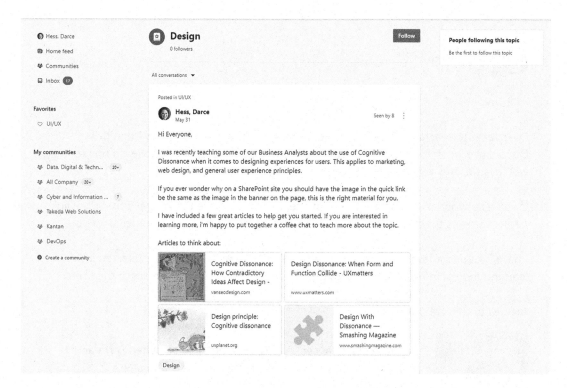

Figure 15-14. *Topic page within Yammer*

If other users are following the topic within Yammer, you will also see them appear in the right column. This will help you discover other people within your organization that are interested in that topic or may have worked on projects related to it.

Microsoft Teams

Microsoft Teams will surface Viva Topics in the same formats that you see inside of SharePoint. The topic is highlighted within posts and, when hovered on, you will see the topic card appear as shown in Figure 15-15. This will allow your users to have a consistent topic experience no matter where they are working from.

Figure 15-15.   *Topic highlighted in Team post*

You can also pin Viva Topics to the app bar in Microsoft Teams. This will enable you to view the Viva Topic Center within Teams. You can see recommended topics that you may be interested and content associated with topics as shown in Figure 15-16.

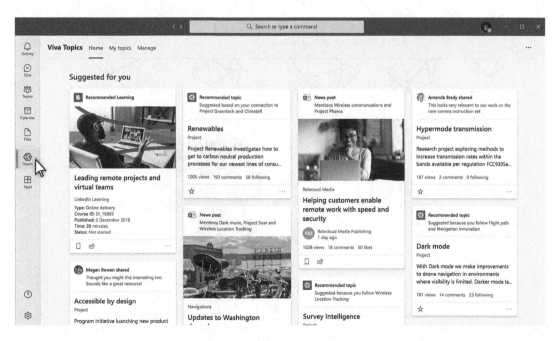

Figure 15-16.   *Viva Topic Center in Teams*

Topic search will show the Viva Topics when you search from within the context of the application you're in such as Microsoft Word as seen below in Figure 15-17.

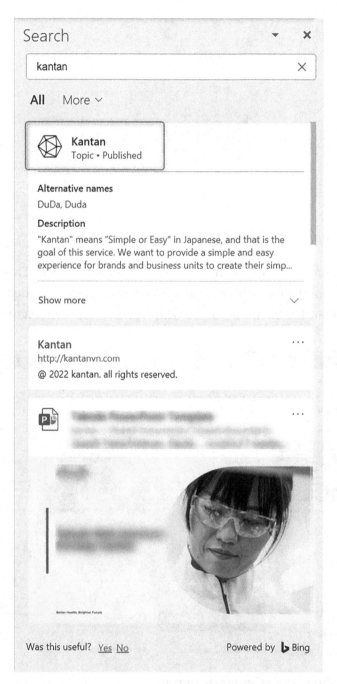

Figure 15-17. Topic search

Topic Center

The Topic Center is where topics are curated and maintained for the organization. User can come to the topic center and search for a specific topic or discovery topics. Below, in Figure 15-18, you will view the Topic Center.

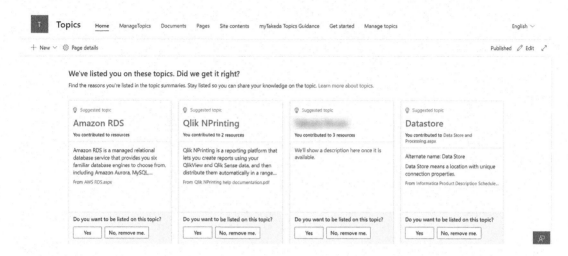

Figure 15-18. *A view of the Topic Center*

Language Support

Microsoft currently provides English language support; however, support for Spanish, French, and German are on the roadmap to be supported soon.

Summary

In this chapter, you learned how to identify potential topics in your organization, create, manage, and remove Topic pages in the Topic Center. You learned where and how users can view and interact with topics and understand the permissions behind Viva Topics.

PART V

Microsoft Viva Insights

To measure and track employee engagement, the Viva Insights module provides managers, employees, and leaders with the insights and recommendations to thrive, supplying personal insights that boost well-being and manager insights into work patterns to prevent burnout and stress.

CHAPTER 16

Employee Well-being

Product Overview

Microsoft Viva Insights provides you with personalized recommendations to help you do your work. The goal is to supply insights into building better work habits, like protecting focus time during the day for uninterrupted, individual work. Viva Insights provides three different aspects: an end user's dashboard, a manager's dashboard, and a leader dashboard. For end users, the dashboard focusses on building new productive habits. It shows reminders to praise colleagues or block focus time in your calendar.

© D'arce Hess, Albert-Jan Schot, Tracy van der Schyff 2023
D. Hess et al., *Getting Started with Microsoft Viva*, https://doi.org/10.1007/978-1-4842-8590-9_16

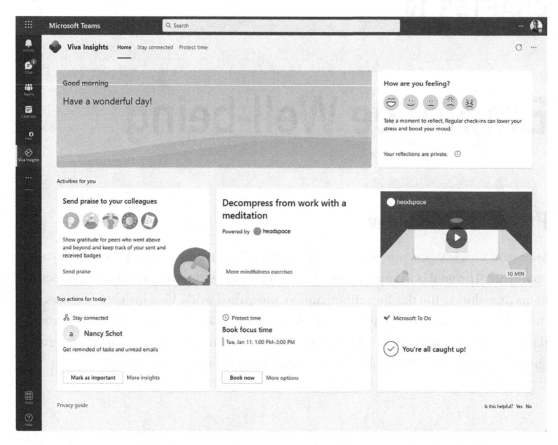

Figure 16-1. *Viva Insights dashboard for end users in Microsoft Teams*

For managers or team leads, the dashboard provides team insights as well as suggestions on how your habits as a manager or team lead impacts the team. It leverages the same Microsoft Teams app, but if you are identified as a manager, you will have the My Team option available.

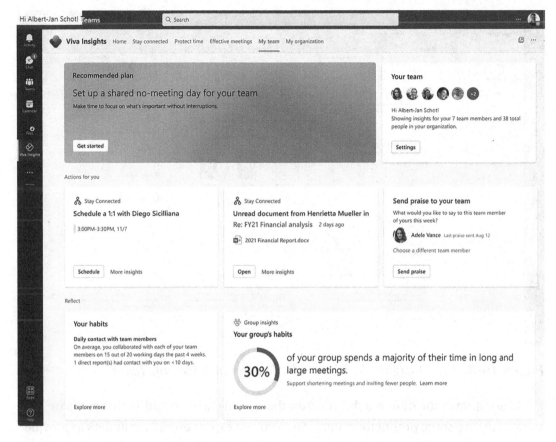

Figure 16-2. *Viva Insights dashboard for managers in Microsoft Teams*

For business leaders, an additional dashboard is available, the My Organization dashboard. This dashboard focusses more on patterns and trends and supplies a global organization overview that tracks different metrics over different teams as well.

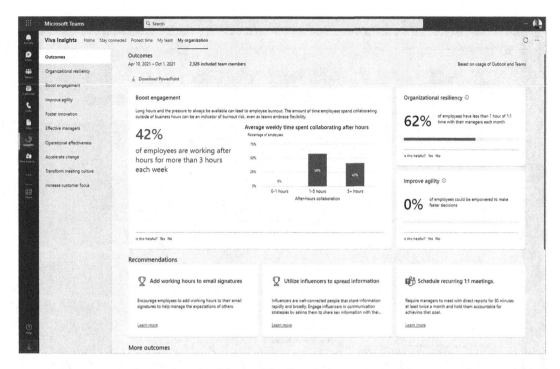

Figure 16-3. *Viva Insights dashboard for leaders in Microsoft Teams*

In addition to the different dashboards, there is an Outlook Add-in that surfaces some of the personal productivity data. And you can expect e-mail reminders to provide insights.

Privacy

With any solution that tracks data, privacy becomes a hot topic. So, Microsoft Viva Insights is designed to protect privacy. Any Personal insights are visible only to the individual; you can only access your personal insights and those insights cannot be accessed by anyone else in the organization. For manager and leader insights, no new personally identifiable information about you or anybody else in your organization is tracked. The insights and actions are based on information generated by you and your organization just by going about your regular workday. Your insights are based on information that you already have access to, but can't quickly aggregate without help. The information that is stored to provide the dashboards with data is stored in your Exchange Online mailbox, so all security policies that are implemented by Exchange are helping in securing the Viva Insights information. Microsoft Viva complies with the General Data Protection Regulation (GDPR), and if you no longer want to use Viva Insights, Microsoft honors your request to export, delete, or restrict the processing of personal data. As an organization, you are in control as to whether Microsoft Viva is turned on by default, turned off, or cannot be used at all.

The Modules

The Microsoft Viva solution consists of several different modules or components. It provides insights using several dashboards, integrations in Microsoft Teams and Microsoft Outlook, and provides e-mail reminders. If you acquire an additional license (Viva Insights Capacity) you can also create your own advanced analysis or use custom integrations. The main components that make up Microsoft Viva are the following:

- Personal insights
- Manager insights
- Leader insights
- Viva Insights Capacity

Personal Insights

The Microsoft Viva Personal Insights are more focused on providing a set of controls than on providing an overview of your productivity. These functionalities are available for anyone with a Microsoft 365 plan that includes Exchange Online! On your personal dashboard, you will find several components or widgets that will help you:

- How are you feeling: by reflecting on your day so far, you can see a trend in how you are feeling.
- Send Praise: a reminder to send acclaim either publicly in teams, or in a private chat. A way to keep meaningful connections with your colleagues.
- Find your flow state: a guided meditation way to clear your head and improve breathing to help reduce stress.
- Stay connected: an AI-based reminder to provide you with task and meeting suggestions.

- Protect time: provides reminder to book focus time to achieve your goals.

- To-do: a quick-glance overview of your upcoming tasks and reminders to take on future tasks.

As the Personal Insights dashboard uses AI to decide what widgets you would see, it could be that during the day the order of those widgets switch. Using the Viva Insights dashboard, you can turn on additional functionality like the reflection schedule to track your emotions or a virtual commute to wrap up your day. Personal insights are also available using the Microsoft Viva Insights Home.

In addition to these dashboards, there is a set of e-mails. By default, you are provided with a Briefing e-mail and Digest e-mail in Outlook. The Briefing e-mail is a daily reminder that helps you stay in control by providing an overview of outstanding commitments and follow-ups, while the Digest e-mail provides a monthly summary about your work patterns.

The final piece of personal insights is an Outlook add-in that helps you with inline recommendations. It can track your e-mail and open rates, provides reminders to follow up on requests, and can notify you of important documents or delay e-mail delivery to fit the majority of the recipients' working hours.

Manager Insights

If you are flagged as a manager in the Azure Active Directory, you will have an extra possibility in the Viva Insights Teams application. The My Team option shows you the trend of employee engagement and team effectiveness. As a manager you have control over who is in your team, and while the initial setup is done using the Azure Active Directory manager attribute, you can add or remove team members to your liking. However, you will only be recognized as a manager if you have the Viva Insights license assigned to your account.

With that license, you also get more insights into working habits, including how your habits influence your team. With this, you get some options for advanced insights and reminders to block one-on-ones with your team members.

Leader Insights

If you have a Microsoft Viva license and are assigned the proper permissions, you can also get Leader Insights. As a business leader, the dashboard provides you with an overview of several key metrics that identify the work culture and how that affects well-being. Metrics around work-life balance and team cohesion will provide insights and research backed results.

Analysis Capabilities

When your organization has purchased a Viva Insights Capacity license, you get additional options to work with the data that is tracked in Microsoft Viva. With research-backed information regarding work productivity and business performance in your organization and the option to extend the data with surveys or CRM data, you can write complex queries to discover trends. Using the data available with Viva Insights Capacity, you can track your own plans as well as use prebuilt functions to create complex analyses. Prebuilt functions, that is, text mining, clustering, or using R (a language and environment for statistical computing and graphics) to process the data.

Integration

The Viva Insights Capacity can be explored using the R package as well as using Power BI. Both tools can be used to create custom reports, combine different sets of data, and create complex integrations. The Viva Insights also supplies a Power BI dashboard that allows you to track manager effectiveness. This dashboard data can also be used to create your own reports. In both cases, the tools are focused on data scientists and not on the typical end user.

Metrics

Viva Insights uses two distinct types of metrics. Readily available metrics like e-mails you send. And computed metrics like colleagues you often interact with.

Based on Your Work

Each building block of Viva Insights uses your work to aggregate and gather the required information. Based on your meetings, interactions using e-mail, teams, or Yammer, or documents you collaborate on, it generates a network of people and your interactions. These interactions are used to highlight people you could send praise to. Or just to make sure you stay connected, by pointing you to promises you made to people and might not have kept. All metrics that are based on your work can be grouped into several categories:

- **Person metrics:** what you are doing in the Microsoft 365 environment; sending e-mail, using Teams, working on documents

- **Peer comparison metrics:** same as person metrics but de-identified to compare to peers

- **Meeting metrics:** what is happening in meetings: who joins and are attendees paying attention to the meeting

- **Group-to-group metrics:** what is happening in Microsoft Teams; how many chat messages are sent, meetings run and how many attendees join Team meetings

- **Person-to-person metrics:** what are you doing in Microsoft Teams, sending chat messages or e-mails

- **Network metrics:** calculations based on your work that determine the links and influence you have in the organization

Questionnaires About Feelings

Research has shown that just the act of reflecting improves your well-being. Using that insight, one of the building blocks asks you to provide how you are feeling by selecting an emoji. This data is stored and only visible for you. No one else knows or can see what you chose.

Stay in Control

Besides the dashboards, Viva Insights provides you with tools to stay in control. Blocking focus time or a Virtual Commute in your calendar, controls to send praise to other people. Or a reminder to delay delivery when sending an e-mail to make sure it is delivered during the working hours of the recipient, are just a few of the examples that you can leverage with Viva Insights.

Block Time

You can protect your time in two ways using Viva Insights. Using focus time, you can block a part of the day to focus on a specific task or action. Another way is to use the Virtual Commute at the end of the day to wrap up the day. While the reminders and signals that are used to remind are private, choosing to block time during the day might be visible for colleagues and coworkers if you share your calendar.

Praise People

Using the praise functionality, you can recognize contributions of your coworkers. When sending praise, you can send it as a private chat or as a wider conversation in a Teams channel. Sending praise sent in a Teams channel is available for all those who are members of that team. When sending praise AI is used to decide who you have been working with to provide you with suggestions. Of course, you can select any user you like to recognize contributions.

Briefing

To stay in control of your calendar and daily work, the Briefing e-mail sends you a reminder that contains an overview of outstanding requests or follow-ups that you might have missed. It provides a trigger to make sure you block focus time or catch-up with your team if you are a manager or a team lead. These triggers and reminders can help you retain focus and deliver on your promises.

All options available to you to stay in control are described in the following chapters.

CHAPTER 17

Licensing Viva Insights and Viva Insights Capacity

Viva Insights provides several different modules and components to provide insights and there are three distinct licensing options. As part of Microsoft 365 plans that contains Exchange Online, you have several Viva Insights features at your disposal. On top of those "free" features, you can buy the Viva Insights license that provides additional features for even more insights and controls. Finally, as an addition to the Viva Insights itself there is the Microsoft Viva Insights Capacity feature. This feature allows you to work with more advanced analytics.

All Viva Insights licenses require an Exchange Online license as well.

Insights by MyAnalytics

The Microsoft 365 Plans that provides you with Exchange Online serves as the basis for Viva Insights. You get access to the basics, including several personal insights with one of the following licenses:

- Microsoft 365 E3
- Microsoft 365 Business
- Microsoft 365 A3 for faculty and students
- Office 365 E3
- Office 365 E1
- Office 365 A3 for faculty and students
- Office 365 E3 Developer
- Office 365 G3

179

© D'arce Hess, Albert-Jan Schot, Tracy van der Schyff 2023
D. Hess et al., *Getting Started with Microsoft Viva*, https://doi.org/10.1007/978-1-4842-8590-9_17

- Business Premium

- Business Essentials

With any of these licenses, you get access to the Viva Dashboard in Microsoft Teams and the Viva Home dashboard. Early 2022, you can still access the My Analytics dashboard as well; this dashboard, however, will become part of Microsoft Viva.

Besides several dashboards, you also get access to the monthly digest e-mail and daily briefing e-mail. And the last bit of goodies is the Outlook add-in. Yet not all functionality in the Outlook add-in is available. Three of the options are only available with a premium license or add-on license.

- Read-status features

- Shorten a meeting

- Delay delivery plan

These premium functions are part of the Viva Insights add-on license, either Microsoft Viva Insights, formerly Workplace Analytics, or one of the following:

- Microsoft 365 E5

- Microsoft 365 E5 without Audio Conferencing

- Office 365 Enterprise E5

- Office 365 Nonprofit E5

- Office 365 G5

- Microsoft 365 A5 for faculty and students

- Office 365 A5 for faculty and students

Viva Insights Add-On

The premium functions are part of the Viva Insights add-on license called Microsoft Viva Insights, formerly Workplace Analytics. With this premium license, you get access to the Manager and Leader insights in Microsoft Teams and Viva Home, and additional insights in the Personal Insights. Assigning the license is all there is from a requirement perspective, but to determine your team members, the Azure AD is leveraged to get all users that have a manager assigned. You can extend this information by selecting members manually when setting up the manager insights. You also require at least ten licensed members before the My Team insights are properly filled. This ensures that you won't be able to translate any data to personal accounts and the reports stay anonymous.

The Leader Insights are provided in an organization dashboard available in the Microsoft Teams App. The insights consist of a broader range of metrics in a company-wide overview. Metrics like after-hours collaboration fuel insights into the work-life balance, and external collaboration metrics are used to provide insights into the customer focus of the organization.

Viva Insights Capacity Feature

On top of the Viva Insights add-on, you can also acquire the Microsoft Viva Insights Capacity. With this separate license, you can write custom reports based on the available metrics using both Power BI and an R-script library. With this data, you can discover trends and networks within the organization with built-in safeguards around personal privacy. The Viva Insights Capacity feature focusses heavily on the complex data that is gathered in Viva Insights and is primarily a tool for analysts to explore this data.

Preparing Your Environment

Before assigning licenses, you must decide the default setup. Without additional configuration, Microsoft Viva is turned on by default. Resulting in the scenario where assigning licenses will allow those users to interact with Viva Insights but also automatically send a welcome email and the weekly email. As an administrator, there are controls to configure these settings. The environment can be configured as follows:

- **Default on** – For all your users, Viva Insights is turned on; users (with a license) can turn off the Viva Insights features (the default option). This setting does not require any changes or configuration on the tenant.

- **Default off** – For all users, Viva Insights is turned off; users (with a license) can turn on the Viva Insights features. To change these settings, a Microsoft 365 Administrator must sign into the admin center and navigate to **Settings – Org Settings – Services – Microsoft Viva Insights** to turn off Viva Insights settings. In the services overview you can also find the option **Briefing email from Microsoft Viva** where you can configure the use of the Briefing email.

- **Mixed** – You decide what users receive the default on, and the default off experience. Setting up any mixed mode requires basic PowerShell understanding. Using the Exchange Online cmdlets, you the following cmdlets:

  - Get-MyAnalyticsFeatureConfig to retrieve the user configuration

  - Set-MyAnalyticsFeatureConfig to update a user's setting. Provides both an opt-in and an opt-out option using the -PrivacyMode parameter. With the -Feature parameter, you get to choose what features (all, add-in, dashboard, digest-email) are enabled or disabled.

  - Keep in mind that only disabling the digest-email feature users still can expect the Briefing Email.

Using the mixed mode, you can also configure all features to be turned off by default with an optional Opt-in if your use case requires this. There are additional commands available to set more specific settings. Set-MyAnalyticsFeatureConfig allows you to enable or disable headspace and Set-UserBriefingConfig lets you enable or disable the briefing e-mails.

Keep in mind that turning off or on any of the Organization settings can take up to 24 hours to take effect. When setting up a blank new tenant, it can even take up to 48 hours before all components are in place.

Each user thus must have a proper Viva Insights license, something that can be added through the Microsoft 365 Admin center or PowerShell when using the Exchange Online cmdlets. For the access to premium features of Viva Insights, users must be assigned the **Insights Administrator** or **Insights Business Leader** in the Azure Active Directory.

CHAPTER 18

Personal Insights

The goal of Personal insights of Viva is to help you identify your work habits and to provide actionable insights as blocking focus time or as simple as to follow up on promises made. Personal insights are available within the context of your work. Whether you are working in Teams or Outlook, both productivity tools provide you with the insights to help you. Viva Insights provides you with three important opportunities:

- **Dashboards:** available in both Teams, Outlook, and the Viva Home so you can get the insights into your work habits.

- **Actions:** from the Teams and Outlook integration so you can book focus time or praise your colleagues for work well done without leaving the tools at hand.

- **Triggers:** reminders and digests around your work.

You will also encounter some functionality still being called MyAnalytics; early 2022 MyAnalytics is still being transitioned into Viva Insights and for a large part already shows up there. However, a few of the settings and configuration still are part of MyAnalytics.

With Personal Insights, you get insights regardless of your workload. If you work in Microsoft Teams, you get to use the Teams App, but if you are in Outlook, you can use the Add-in. All captured data is available regardless of the collaboration tool you prefer. And with the Viva Insights Home, you can always resort to a website available from your browser.

Setup

By default, most of your users will have basic access to the Personal Insights as described in the previous chapter. Depending on the tenant configuration chosen, you can decide who has access to what.

© D'arce Hess, Albert-Jan Schot, Tracy van der Schyff 2023
D. Hess et al., *Getting Started with Microsoft Viva*, https://doi.org/10.1007/978-1-4842-8590-9_18

Microsoft Teams Setup

To make sure users can discover the Personal Insights in Teams, you can, as a Teams Service Administrator, configure the Teams apps setup policy to include Viva Insights as a pinned app.

From the Teams Admin center, a Teams Service Administrator can configure the global app setup policy or create additional setup policies to match business needs.

1.   Browse to `https://admin.teams.microsoft.com/` as a Teams Administrator.

2.   From the left navigation, open Teams apps and select the Setup policies.

3.   In the Setup Policies, either add a new policy or edit the Global (Org-wide default) policy.

4.   Click the button Add apps to search for Viva Insights.

5.   Select Viva Insights and click on Add to add it to the list of Pinned Apps.

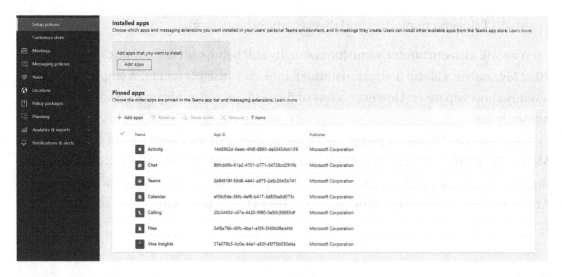

Figure 18-1. *Teams Admin center app policies*

Once an administrator has pinned the Viva Insights apps for all users, it will show up in all Teams clients and users can navigate to their dashboards.

Exchange Online Setup

The Outlook add-in is available by default for all users. As an Exchange Administrator with the Org Marketplace Apps role, you can disable the add-in. To disable the add-in, navigate to the Exchange Admin Center and under organization select Add-ins. From the Add-ins screen you can edit the default settings, making it mandatory or optional or remove the add-in to prevent users from using it.

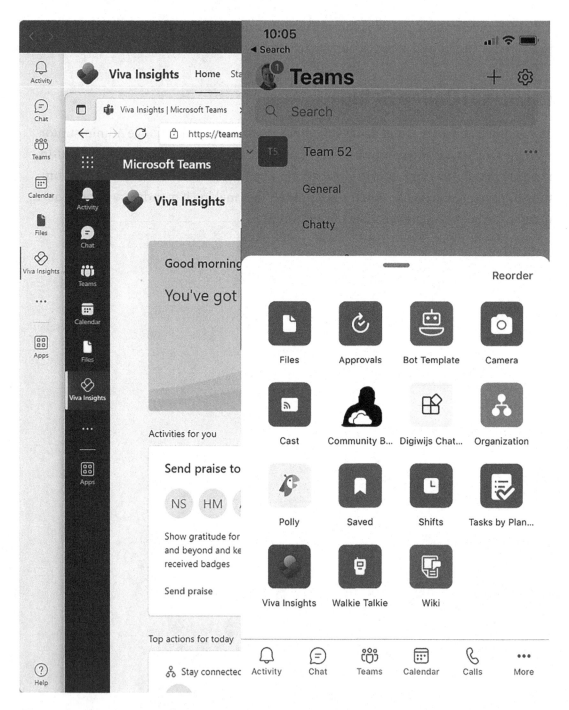

Figure 18-2. *Viva Insights in Teams*

Privacy

Viva Personal Insights uses your personal data to generate insights, but it is important to note that it does not allow tracking or profiling of user profiles. Personal Insights are stored in your Exchange Online Mailbox and only you have access to that Exchange Online mailbox, and thus to that data.

Personal insights and actions in the Viva Insights app are based on your Exchange Online Mailbox data. For example, e-mails being sent or calendar invites you accepted. Any data that is used for manager or leader insights is anonymized or depersonalized, making sure that it cannot lead back to personal identifiable information.

If your organization chooses to use Viva Insights and you do not want to use the Personal Insights, you can at any moment opt out using the following steps.

1. Browse to `https://insights.viva.office.com/`

2. From the top navigation bar, click on the gear icon and select settings.

3. Click the "**Generate insights based on my Microsoft 365 usage to help me be more productive**" toggle to opt-out.

Once switched off, it can take up to a week before everything is processed, but no additional work data is captured.

If at any point you do want to opt-in again, you can navigate to the same dashboard and toggle the switch to opt-in again.

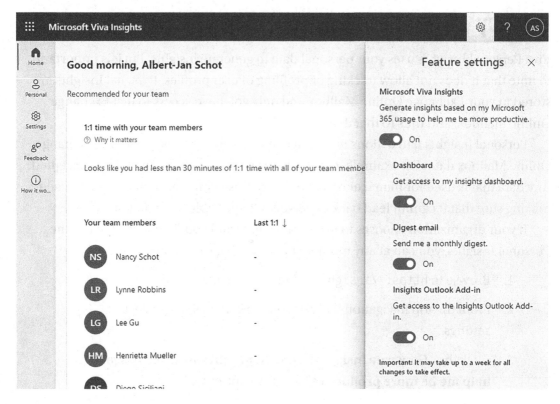

Figure 18-3. *Opt-out of Viva Insights*

Key Principles

- Only you have access to your personal insights.

- Your data is stored and protected in your Exchange Online Mailbox.

- Insights aggregated at a higher level for managers will never show personal identifiable information other than what is publicly available in Outlook and Teams.

- You can opt-out at any time.

Microsoft Teams App

The Microsoft Viva Insights app in Microsoft Teams shows a personalized dashboard with your insights. All data showed is personal and private and the data is not available for managers or system administrators.

Opening the Microsoft Teams app shows a home page that highlights most of the Viva Personal Insights features. The app offers a navigation bar to navigate between different features and an overview of several cards highlights some of these features.

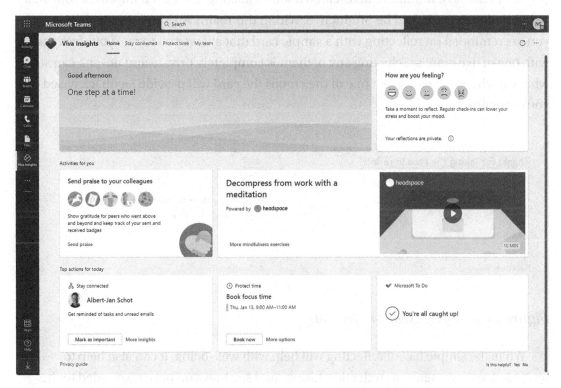

***Figure 18-4.** Viva Insights Teams overview*

The different cards on the page show quick actions or insights. Divided in three sections, you will find the first section to hold a welcome message or notifications to alert you to events such as Lunch or the Virtual Commute. The card's color will change depending on the different status. Besides the welcome message, you are asked to reflect on your current mood. The second section focusses on activities or actions you can take, praising colleagues and meditate using Headspace. The last section is built around actions for the working day. It shows reminders to connect with colleagues, suggest protecting time to focus and shows open To Do's.

Reflect

Incorporate regular reflections on how you are feeling is a great way to learn more about yourself. There is a multitude of research about reflecting and how it improves your well-being, ability to learn, and be productive. Within the Teams App and Viva Insights Home, you are reminded on reflecting with a simple card that allows you to rate your feelings with one of five emojis. Selecting any of them is completely private and no-one can see what you choose. If you select one of the emojis the card will provide feedback based on your selection.

Figure 18-5. *Viva Insights reflections*

While the simple fact of reflecting will help with well-being, it can also help to look back, you can see your reflection history and see how you have responded to the questions over time.

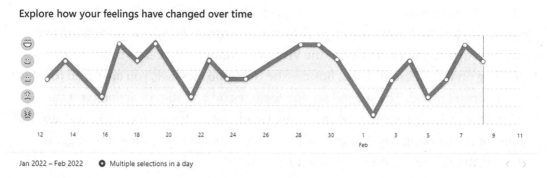

Figure 18-6. *Viva Insights Reflections history*

From the history screen, you can directly navigate to the settings page to set up reminders for reflection. Once turned on, you can schedule what days of the week you do want to receive reflection reminders. Not only during the work week but any day that you feel would be the best moment to reflect can be used to get a notification.

Setting up a reminder will send the notification in a 30-minute window of your desired time. Setting it to 09:00 am will remind you between 08:45 am and 09:15 am.

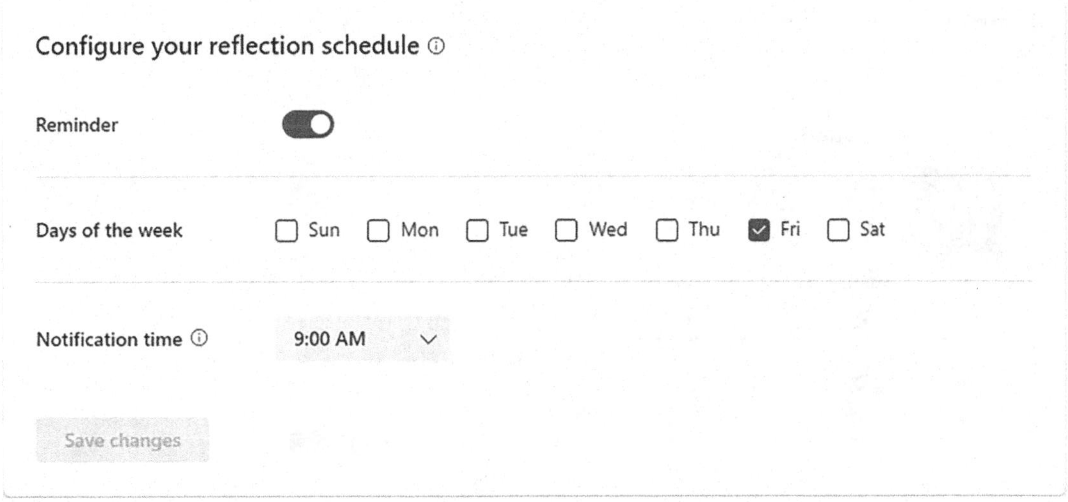

Configure your reflection schedule ⓘ

Reminder   ●─○

Days of the week   ☐ Sun ☐ Mon ☐ Tue ☐ Wed ☐ Thu ☑ Fri ☐ Sat

Notification time ⓘ   9:00 AM   ⌄

Save changes

Figure 18-7. *Viva Insights Reflections settings*

If you ignore the reminder during the day, you will get a message that the reminder is expired if you try to use that reminder to reflect. You can navigate back to the Teams App or Viva Insights Home any time to submit a reflection. Any submission on one those pages are independent of your reminder; even though you might have just submitted your input, you will still receive a reminder.

Send Praise

To recognize contributions made by colleagues or team members, you can use the Send Praise functionality. Sending praise can be done through the Teams App, as a Message Extension and from the Viva Insights Home page.

Sending a Praise Message is straightforward, you need to identify the colleague you want to recognize, pick the appropriate icon, and send a short message. When sending praise, you can choose the message to be delivered in a private chat or as a Teams message for the whole team to see. You can only select teams you are both a member of to prevent praise messages to be shared to teams the recipient has no access to and thus misses the praise.

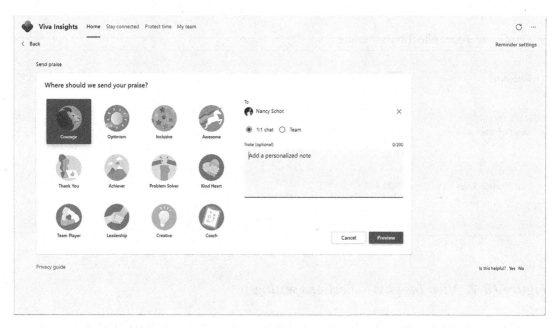

Figure 18-8. *Viva Insights sending praise*

You can also send Praise from the context of a chat. In any active conversation in Microsoft Teams, you can find the Praise icon. If the icon is missing, make sure to click the three ellipsis and search for the word Praise to activate it in the chat.

Figure 18-9. *Viva Insights sending praise as a message*

Selecting the app will walk you through the same process except that it will automatically share the praise in the current chat. You cannot share a praise to a whole team. Once the praise message is sent, the recipient will receive a notification.

Like with the reflect functionality, you can setup a reminder schedule. By doing so, you are presented with notification. Clicking the notification redirects you to the praise feature directly.

Figure 18-10. *Viva Insights Praise reminder notification*

By building a habit of recognizing coworkers, you can build a positive culture within your organization or team. It makes colleagues feel appreciated and enforces good behavior.

Virtual Commute

By default, no Virtual Commute schedule or reminder is set up, and the Teams App will only show you a "Wrap up your day" in the first card on the dashboard. The message shows up 30 minutes before the end of your workday as scheduled in your Outlook. The same option can be found on the Protect time tab in the top navigation. You can, however, set up your own schedule. As with the Reflect and Praise functionality, you can configure a reminder schedule, and with those reminders, notifications will appear in a 30-minute window of your desired time.

If you get the notification or click start, the virtual commute takes you through four steps to make sure you can wrap up your work.

- **Review tasks** shows all open tasks in Microsoft To-Do that have a due date or reminder date set today. You mark tasks as done if you finished them or update the reminder date to make sure there are no loose ends or forgotten actions. There also is an option to add new tasks for anything that might pop up and is important enough to capture. Updating or Adding tasks will reflect in the Briefing e-mail and the To-Do card on the homepage.

- **Preview next day's calendar** shows an overview of the upcoming meetings for the next day. It helps you prepare and make some final decisions on the schedule of the next day. You can RSVP or delete meetings if you have conflicting obligations.

- **Reflect** using the same experience as the card on the homepage as part of your virtual commute you are asked to reflect on your day.

- **Headspace** is used to finalize. You can watch a short, guided meditation video to disconnect after a days' worth of work.

Headspace

The headspace provides a curated set of guided meditations and focus music. You can click more mindfulness exercises to start your day, with focus or relax a bit when wrapping up your day. All clips are relatively short so, in just a few minutes a day, you can build in a meditation habit.

If you are using the Focus music, it is recommended to pop out the Viva Insights app so you can keep using Microsoft Teams to collaborate while listening to music. You can pop out the app by right clicking on the Viva Insights icon and selecting Pop out app.

Figure 18-11. *Pop out the Viva Insights app*

Stay Connected

Stay connected is the overview of people you work with and acts as a reminder to stay in touch or to follow up on actions. The dashboard provides several insights based on your collaboration patterns and it recognizes your top collaborators. You can choose to pin those collaborators to give them additional importance.

Meeting Reminders

For your top collaborators pinned or not, you can easily schedule a 1:1 meeting reminder. Staying connected can be hard; so, Viva Insights will send a reminder if you did not have a 1:1 with the colleague in the specified time frame. You can set the time frame to from weekly, bi-weekly to monthly or turn it off completely.

Meeting Suggestions

If you do receive a meeting reminder, you can use the card to quickly schedule a meeting using the available dates or use the View calendar for other items to schedule a meeting that better fits your schedule.

Figure 18-12. *Viva Insights meeting suggestion*

If there happens to be a conflict and the meeting is double booked, Viva Insights sends a new reminder to reschedule the meeting.

Outstanding Tasks

Whenever you promise something in an e-mail, it is easy to lose track of those commitments. Based on the last 14 days of e-mail you sent and requests you got from colleagues, Viva Insights scans for the following:

- **Commitments** – things you promised or committed to do

- **Requests** – things asked of you

- **Follow-ups** – something that you were asked for from someone else in an e-mail

Unread Documents Shared with You

Any document that is shared with you through OneDrive, SharePoint, or an e-mail that you have not read yet will show up here. You can quickly open the document and read up on what you missed.

Mentions

With Microsoft Teams, mentions can become overwhelming if you get too many of them. With this view, you can quickly get a hold of mentions made by your top collaborators and pinned contacts.

Upcoming Meetings

In case you have not read your e-mail, the upcoming meeting shows any meeting that you still have to RSVP on.

Protect Time

Anyone knows distractions get in the way of getting things done and research backs this up. Getting distracted requires you to spend additional energy in getting back in the focus zone, draining your energy. Having uninterrupted work is the best way to focus on complex challenges in your important projects. With Viva Insights, you can quickly block focus time in your calendar. Blocking just a few hours a day will help you achieve more progress. Whenever you schedule focus time, Viva Insights will make sure that all chats and calls are muted so you won't be distracted.

Settings

A lot of the settings you can do in the Teams App are provided as a guided experience. Opening the app for the first time provides a first run experience asking you for input. Most of the cards trigger you to provide some settings. Once those settings are configured, you can always navigate to the three ellipsis and select settings to edit existing settings.

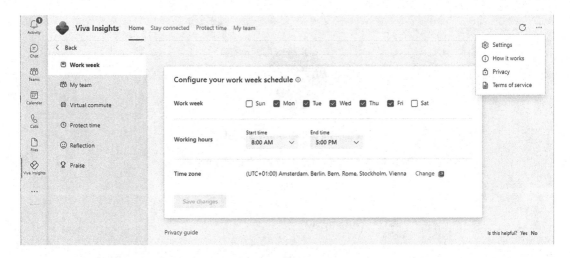

Figure 18-13. *Viva Insights Teams App settings*

The settings page allows you to change your work schedule or any of the configured notification reminders for Virtual commute, reflection, and praise.

Outlook Add-In

With the Viva Insights available in Outlook, most of the features you find in the Teams Dashboard are available. As well as some features focused on e-mail scenarios only. Opening the App in the Outlook client or Outlook Web App can be done by clicking the three ellipsis when selecting an e-mail and selecting the Viva Insights app. When opening the app, you can expect several cards to show.

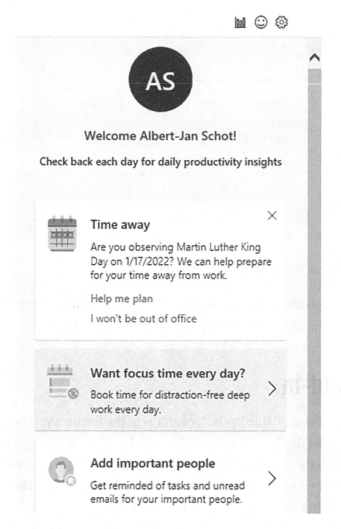

Figure 18-14. *Viva Insights in Outlook*

Time Away

The time away feature helps you in checking of a checklist when you take time off. It uses public holidays as a reminder to book time off. Booking time through this interface helps you by composing an automatic reply (out of office). Sending an e-mail or calendar invite to your collaborators. Resolve all your meetings during that period. And finally, allowing you to book time to focus to make sure you can catch up with whatever you might have missed.

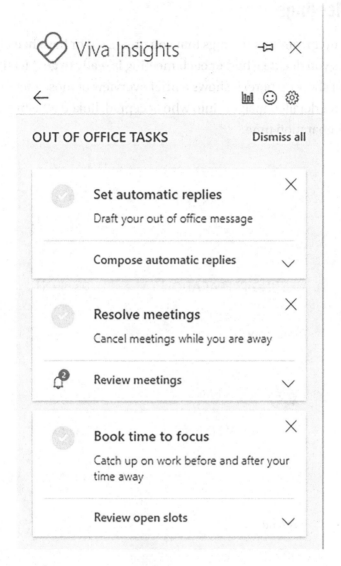

Figure 18-15. *Schedule your time away*

Focus Time

Booking time to focus uses the same functionality as Protect Time in the Viva Insights in Microsoft Teams. You can use it to block time in your calendar and to get things done. Using the Outlook integration, you can automatically book the current week and the week ahead.

Upcoming Meetings

A brief overview of upcoming meetings that you organized or have been invited to. This insight helps you decide whether each meeting is ready to go. Meetings without attendees will not show up here. It shows a brief overview of those meetings and, as an organizer, you have detailed insights into who accepted, linked attachments, and the option to book preparation time.

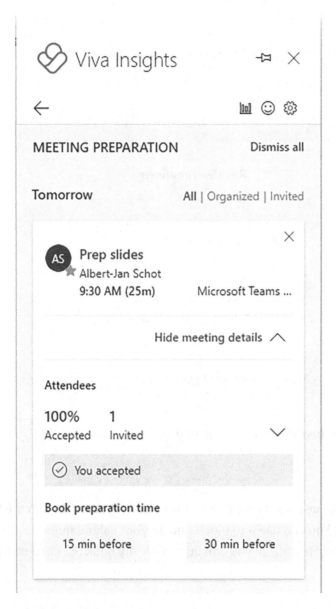

Figure 18-16. *Upcoming meetings*

Set Lunch Hours

Studies prove that taking a lunch break allows recharge and refocus. New users therefore are presented with the option to automatically block an hour for lunch each day. The card will disappear if not used, but you can always change the settings in the settings pane afterwards.

Meeting Suggestions

Like with the Viva Insights app in Teams, you can stay in touch with top collaborators by scheduling 1:1 meetings. Based on your important people, you are presented with reminders if you are falling out of touch. With this card, you can quickly book a meeting to stay in touch.

Outstanding Tasks

Like the Viva Insights Outstanding task card in Teams, the Outlook version surfaces your outstanding commitments based on e-mails you have sent in the last 14 days.

Unread Documents

Any document that is shared with you through OneDrive, SharePoint, or an e-mail that you have not read yet will show up here. You can quickly open the document and read up on what you missed.

Track E-mail and Document Open Rates

Insights can also be used to track e-mail and document open rates; however, there are a few requirements before tracking takes place. The goal is to provide insights as to whether your document or e-mail is read, but to guard the privacy of users not all e-mails or documents qualify. When sending an e-mail, the first requirement is that there must be at least five internal recipients, as tracking only works for internal accounts. Second is that the open rate must fall in a certain range dependent of the number of recipients, as shown in the following table:

Number of recipients	Open rate
5–10	Minimum: 25%
	Maximum: 75%
11–20	Minimum: 10%
	Maximum: 90%
21+	Minimum: 5%
	Maximum: 95%

In addition to those e-mails sent from a shared mailbox or to a Microsoft 365 group, it is skipped as well. Once an e-mail is sent and it falls within the boundaries, it can take up to 30 minutes before being visible in the report. In addition to these reports, Outlook offers so-called Inline suggestions.

The track e-mail and document open rates does require the Viva Insights license to work.

Inline Suggestions

Inline suggestions in Outlook are notifications that appear in the context of Outlook. They appear when writing or reading e-mails or meeting invitations, by providing insights while you are working on your e-mail or invite you to build healthier working habits.

The most prominent feature with inline suggestions is the Delay Delivery Plan, anytime you are working on an e-mail outside the working hours of your colleague, you get a short notification to consider sending this e-mail later using schedule send.

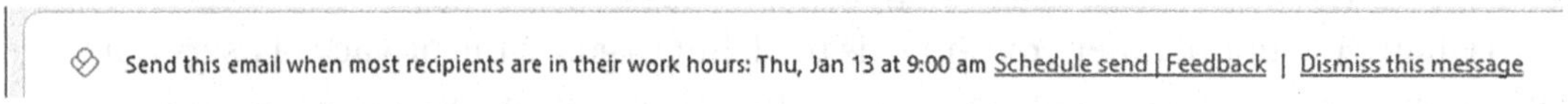

⬦   Send this email when most recipients are in their work hours: Thu, Jan 13 at 9:00 am Schedule send | Feedback | Dismiss this message

Figure 18-17. Delay Delivery Plan

Other inline suggestions you can expect to show up are reminders to shorten a meeting, track your e-mail, or open e-mail rates. And as with the Delay Delivery Plan, these inline suggestions require the Viva Insights (My Analytics) addon license. Inline suggestions about your focus time or outstanding tasks will show up even without that license.

Dashboards
Viva Insights Home

Viva Insights Home is the home page with recommendations like what you can see from Teams or Outlook. It also provides cards that can help in building better habits; reminding you to define your working hours, or establish a no-meeting period. These cards allow you to learn more about a topic, redirecting you to the Microsoft Documentation, essentially taking you away from your dashboard. It is a great way to provide some background, but it can be a bit confusing leaving the dashboard.

Early 2022, some of the settings and configuration still needs to be configured in the MyAnalytics, so selecting the "Personal" tab in the Viva Insights Home will still redirect you to the MyAnalytics homepage; from there, you have additional configuration available.

Focus

While meetings and e-mails are necessary to coordinate your work, too much of those often leave us with little to no time during a workday for focused work. With the focus plan, you are reminded to set up focus time.

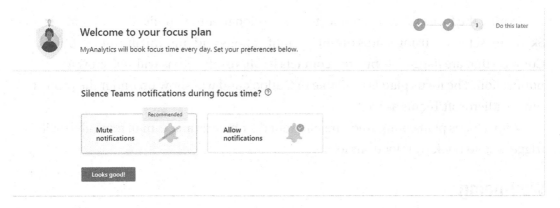

Figure 18-18. *Focus plan setup*

The focus plan setup walks you through a three-step process to set the focus time (one, two, or four hours a day), asks you for your preferred time (morning or afternoon), and checks if you want to mute notifications.

Once the focus plan is created, it will automatically book the next two weeks of focus time and will show any days that require review. Dates that have overlapping meetings with your focus time are flagged. The booking will respect existing meetings if it can find a fitting timeslot. Lunchtime is respected, if possible, by default even if you do not have lunch hours booked.

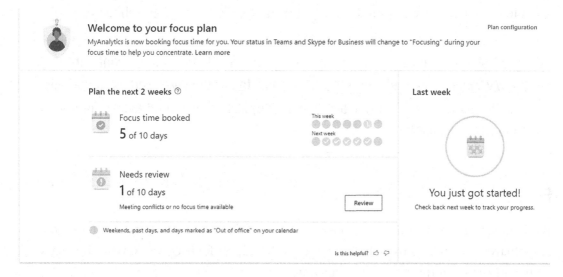

Figure 18-19. *Focus plan results*

During the focus time, if you selected the option to mute notifications, Teams or Skype are set to Focusing status disabling notifications and minimizing interruptions. Contacts that are flagged as priority contacts in Microsoft Teams will still show a notification. The focus plan is available in Outlook and will show up under the protect time in Microsoft Teams as well.

With a focus plan configured, the different dashboards and e-mail reminders will trigger you to book your focus time.

Well-being

The well-being dashboard provides an overview of how well you can disconnect from work outside of working hours. It uses your working hours and checks for collaboration outside these set hours. When sending or reading e-mail, replying to chats or attending meetings outside the normal working hours these days will not count as quiet days. The dashboards show you metrics around these quiet days.

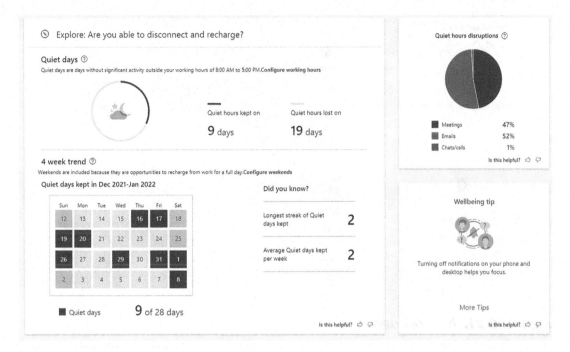

Figure 18-20. *Quiet Days overview*

Having not enough quiet days can be a sign of high levels of stress and increases the risk of burnout. You can use this metric to rethink the number of notifications you allow on your devices or leave your phone at home when going for a walk. Combined with tips to implement the delay delivery plan to be respectful of other people's time off or taking a break yourself can help you with better working habits.

Network

With the network page, you get an overview of people you work with both internally and externally. It shows the most active and total number of people you interacted with. From this dashboard you can add important people, and by doing so MyAnalytics will help with tracking outstanding commitments and tasks. The dashboard also tips around networking or new collaborators.

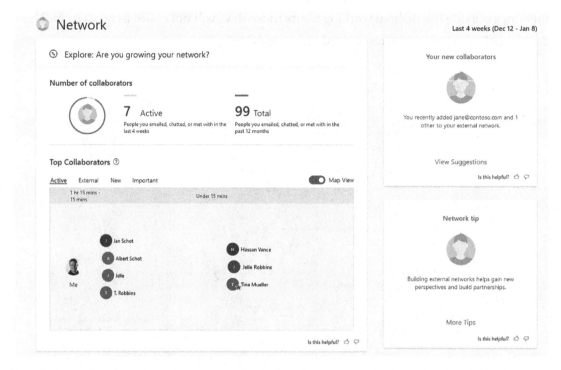

Figure 18-21. *Network overview*

Additional tips you can expect are reminders to set a weekly 1:1 or check in with your manager and make time for networking. The tips aim to improve your network so you can learn from your peers.

Collaboration

The collaboration page focusses on how effectively you spend your time in meetings and e-mail. It shows you a weekly average of your focus time, how much time you spend focusing on meetings, or if you joined meetings on time. You can also find a graph on your communication habits, showing the number of e-mails sent and read, and chats and calls during each period of the day.

Weekly average

Collaboration is the % of time in the last 4 weeks during your working hours. Breakout of your time outside working hours can be found in the Wellbeing section.

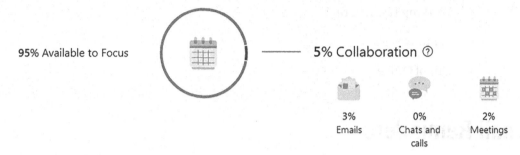

95% Available to Focus ————— 5% Collaboration ⑦

3%
Emails

0%
Chats and calls

2%
Meetings

Communication habits ⑦

How connected are you through the day on email, chats and calls?

You sent 44, read 318 emails and had 1 chat or call in the last 4 weeks

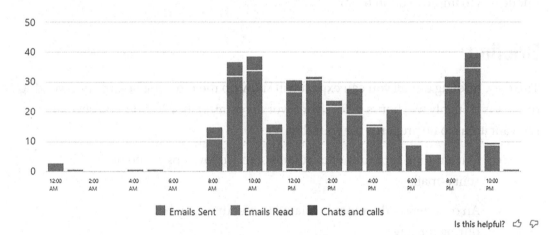

■ Emails Sent   ■ Emails Read   ■ Chats and calls

Is this helpful? 👍 👎

Figure 18-22. *Excerpt of the collaboration overview*

You can find several metrics around the meeting habits. Most of the meetings will show up, except if they fit the exclusion rules:

- Meetings with no other participants but yourself
- Meetings marked as All Day or Private

- Meetings where the Show As is marked as

  - Free

  - Working Elsewhere

  - Tentative

  - Out of Office

Email Reminders

In addition to the reports and dashboards you can navigate to yourself, there are two E-mail reminders you can expect. The briefing e-mail and the digest e-mail. The briefing e-mail is a daily e-mail to get started where you left off yesterday. The digest e-mail is monthly and provides you with a summary of your work patterns and habits and will queue tips to improve upon them.

Briefing

The daily briefing e-mail you can expect will show up the morning before your working day starts (roughly two hours before your workday starts). It will show you several relevant items to be prepared for your day:

- Outstanding commitments, requests and follow-ups based on sent e-mails

- An overview of documents related to meetings you have during the day

- A reminder to block focus time in your calendar

If you open the Outlook Client (Web or Native) to open e-mail you can use the adaptive version the Briefing. With the adaptive version, you can interact with the e-mail inline. Selecting options will directly execute the action for you. When you are using any other app than Outlook, you are presented with an HTML version. This HTML version will show similar information, but interacting with the e-mail will redirect you to the corresponding tools and will not show in-line actions.

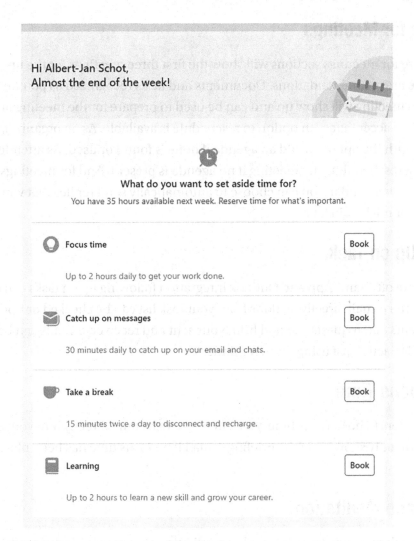

Hi Albert-Jan Schot,
Almost the end of the week!

What do you want to set aside time for?
You have 35 hours available next week. Reserve time for what's important.

Focus time   Book

Up to 2 hours daily to get your work done.

Catch up on messages   Book

30 minutes daily to catch up on your email and chats.

Take a break   Book

15 minutes twice a day to disconnect and recharge.

Learning   Book

Up to 2 hours to learn a new skill and grow your career.

Figure 18-23. *Excerpt of the Briefing e-mail*

Right before the end of the week, you can expect some additional actions to popup in the e-mail with reminders to book breaks, learning moments, or time to catch up on messages. The insights and settings you will receive are based on the same insights as the different dashboards. Sections will only show if there is data available. Sections with no data will be hidden from the e-mail, but additional suggestions around your work habits can appear.

Prepare for Meetings

The prepare for meetings sections will show the first three meetings for the upcoming day if there are recommendations. Documents and tasks recognized as potentially related to a meeting will show up and can be used to prepare for the meeting at hand. In case of low acceptance, an option to reschedule is available. As an organizer, you are presented with the option to add an agenda if none is found or used. As attendee, you can suggest rescheduling the meeting if no agenda is present. And for meetings that overlap in your calendar, you can choose to automatically send replies that you must leave early or might join later.

Follow Up on Tasks

As the Microsoft Teams App and Outlook integration following up on tasks can be done from the e-mail directly, actions from your task list can be checked or updated, commitments and requests scouted from your sent and received e-mails can be added to your To Do action list using these reminders.

Book Focus Time

With reminders to book focus time, you can block focus time directly into your calendar. The card will only show up in the briefing e-mail if no focus time has been blocked for the day.

Headspace Meditation

Headspace allows you to launch a guided meditation to start your day grounded and focused. Clicking the option will try to automatically open the Microsoft Teams application.

Plan Your Week

The last available section is the Plan your week. It shows multiple reminders to book focus time, plan time to catch up on e-mails, and take your breaks. It serves as a reminder to be mindful of your agenda and plan important actions accordingly.

Digests

When assigned a new Viva Insights license, you will receive a welcome notification up to four weeks after being assigned this license. After that, you can expect a monthly update with insights how you spend your days and works and reminders to configure additional Personal Insights settings. It uses the personal insights available in different dashboards to provide you with an overview of those insights. As with all personal insights, everything you see is private to you and cannot be accessed by anyone else.

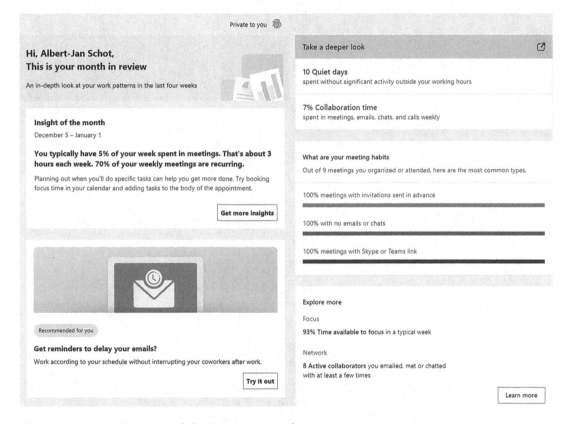

Figure 18-24. *Excerpt of the Digest e-mail*

Conclusion

The goal of personal insights is providing you with the tools to see how the things you do influence your feelings during the day. How choices you make in committing to things will impact others or how you can experience less stress by taking a break.

Depending on the size of your organization, different metrics provide different value. In smaller teams, you will not find results for track e-mail and document open rates, yet you still can get insights into your communication habits to identify when the best time would be to plan uninterrupted focus time. Being mindful of other people's time off can easily achieved using delay delivery and Outlook will let you know whenever it can to do so.

Using Headspace mediation and planned focus time can help anyone to focus on the task at hand with clarity. The personal insights are a great tool in your collaboration box.

CHAPTER 19

Manager Insights

As manager or team lead, you get additional insights when using Viva Insights. These insights typically appear in the existing insight dashboards in Microsoft Teams, Outlook, or the Viva Insights Home, based on your work habits, just like the personal insights would be. As a manager, you get additional sections with information on how your habits impact your team.

With Manager insights, you are provided with a set of unique insights. If you are managing a larger team, Group insights can provide more detail. Manager insights are available for anyone who manages a team, Group insights are only available for teams of ten or more people and everyone on that team must have the Viva Insights license assigned.

Setup

Viva Insights uses Azure Active Directory to determine your direct reports to set up your initial team, but you can choose to override these settings and add additional team members. In case your Azure Active Directory does not have the manager field populated, you can set up your team manually. To use manager insights, the Microsoft Viva Insights license is required.

Group insights are handled differently and are still part of Workplace Analytics. The first step is to navigate to `https://workplaceanalytics.office.com/` and configure additional settings.

> *If you experience an error stating the server is not responding, please validate that you have enabled Workplace Analytics and have a valid license. It sometimes can take up to three days before everything is ready.*

To configure these settings, you need to be assigned the **Insights Administrator** permission. With that permission set, you can configure the Leader and manager settings.

213

© D'arce Hess, Albert-Jan Schot, Tracy van der Schyff 2023
D. Hess et al., *Getting Started with Microsoft Viva*, https://doi.org/10.1007/978-1-4842-8590-9_19

Figure 19-1. *Leader and manager settings*

You can configure whom to show the group insights by selecting all managers or a subset of managers. By changing the team size, you can configure the size of a team a manager is allowed to get group insights for. The measured managers show how many managers qualify with the selected team size. Changing or saving these settings can take over an hour to take effect.

When setting up a new tenant consider that assigning a license can take up to 48 hours before taking effect, but also that gathering manager insights can take up longer. Without this data, you cannot configure or turn on the manager insights and you will be presented with a message that the settings are not ready.

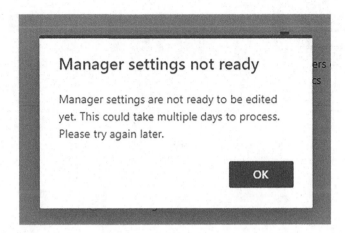

Figure 19-2. *Manager settings on newly created tenant*

For analyst settings, please see the next chapter as it contains details on how to upload organizational data.

Privacy

As a manager, you will not see any incremental information that might lead back to an individual user. All data is either already available in your mailbox or teams. Any other data that is provided is de-personalized. While a metric will show the percentage of people who joined a meeting on time, it will not show the people who were late to that same meeting in the report.

As a manager, you can select, *I don't lead a team* to disable the Manager insights for your account. You can opt-in again at any time.

Team Insights

Your team insights are available at the Viva Insights Home. As a manager or team lead, you are presented with an overview of your team and get regular reminders with call to actions. The goal of these insights and actions is to give an indication of the impact your working habits have on your team; it will not show the habits of your team. Al information on the team insights page is derived from your personal Exchange Online mailbox.

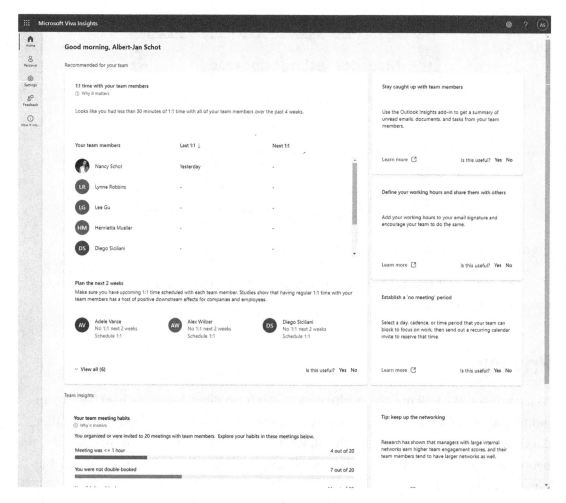

Figure 19-3. *Team insights*

1:1 Reminders

As manager, coaching team members is just one of the many responsibilities you have. With the 1:1 reminder, you are presented with an indication of the time you spent with a team member. Any meeting on your calendar that includes only you and the given team member will count toward the 1:1 time. As a manager, you get a quick overview of last and next 1:1 with each team member. This allows you to quickly schedule and plan the next two weeks.

Quiet Hours Impact

Whenever you work late and check out your tasks by sending e-mails to your team, research suggests that team members take that as a signal that the same behavior is expected from them. Using the Quiet hours impact report provides insights into your activity as a manager outside working hours of your team members. Whenever you send an e-mail outside of the working hours of your team or schedule a meeting, it will count as impact on quiet hours.

When you add new team members, impact on quiet hours will be reflected in the next week.

Team Meeting Habits

Being a manager puts you in a position where team members try to mimic your behavior. Using the Team meeting habits, you are provided with several metrics on how you interact during a meeting.

- Meetings less than an hour

- Meetings that do not overlap with other meetings

- Meetings where you did not multitask (you did read or send e-mails and chats)

- Meetings where you replied to the organizer (RSVP'd)

- Meetings where you joined within five minutes of their scheduled time

These insights are personal and not available for everyone, but as a manager, you can use these insights and the fact that you are a role model within the organization to show healthy work habits.

Group Insights

With manager insights turned on, you can access Group Insights from Teams. These group insights consist of insights based on all employees that report up to you as a manager. By default, the Azure Active Directory is used to determine the hierarchy, but additional data can be uploaded when configuring advanced insights. The insights combine several personal insights into a more aggregated view:

- **Coaching and development:** based on the number of 1:1 meetings between employees and their manager, these insights help you prioritize coaching.

- **Email overload:** the number of hours spent sending and receiving e-mail.

- **After-hours work:** as with personal insights, this aggregates the total number of hours spent outside of normal working hours.

- **Long and large meetings:** any meeting planned for more than an hour is calculated as a long meeting, any meeting that involves more than eight people count as a large meeting. Employees who spend more than 30 percent of their time in long or large meetings are reflected in this metric.

- **Focus time:** employees who have less than 20 hours of available focus time. Focus time is defined as having two or more consecutive hours without meetings.

- **Instant message use:** based on the number of 1:1 instant message vs. the 1:1 e-mails a user sends.

Briefing and Digest E-Mails

When you configure your team members and are recognized as a manager, the Briefing and digest e-mails will show additional information and suggestions.

Digest E-Mail

As a manager, the daily digest e-mail provides reminders regarding your team as part of the Catch up with your team section.

Catch Up with Your Team

With the Catch up with your team section, you can expect several suggestions and actions:

- **Schedule 1:1:** to schedule a 1:1 with team members that you have not scheduled one with.

- **Outstanding tasks:** whenever you promise something in an e-mail and haven't delivered, a reminder will show up.

- **Recent items:** in case you missed and haven't read an e-mail or document, a reminder will ask you to have a look.

Using the Adaptive version, you can schedule or check out outstanding tasks directly.

Conclusion

Using the Manager insights, you are provided with unique insights on how your work habits influence your team members. Without seeing personal collaboration habits, you are presented with recommendations to improve working habits and make it easier to stay in close contact with your team.

CHAPTER 20

Leader Insights

Group and Leader insights terminology are used interchangeably. Yet where group insights concern team members that report to you, leader insights focuses on companywide insights. Each of the dashboards provides a detailed set of best practices matching the report metrics.

Setup

Leader insights uses the same setting as the Group insights. Navigate to `https://workplaceanalytics.office.com/` to configure the additional settings. To configure these settings, you need to be assigned the **Insights Administrator** license. With that license you can configure the Leader and manager settings.

To get access to the Leader insights, you must be assigned either **Insights Administrator**, **Insights Business Leader**, or assigned Workplace Analytics permissions as one of the available roles.

Privacy

The Leader insights use collaboration data from Microsoft 365. All of this data is de-identified to maintain personal privacy in Viva Insights. Optionally, additional organizational data is used for advanced analytics, but that data is also de-identified. Each user can opt out Viva Insights and you can exclude an employee's personal information from being processed by not assigning a Viva Insights license.

The initial data that is captured is the last 13 months of data, and after that it keeps adding data on a weekly interval with up to 27 months' worth of data. After those 27 months, older data is removed in favor of newer data. If a user would leave the organization or its license gets revoked, any data captured will not be removed. If you do want to remove this data, you can request a collaboration data reset through Microsoft support.

© D'arce Hess, Albert-Jan Schot, Tracy van der Schyff 2023
D. Hess et al., *Getting Started with Microsoft Viva*, https://doi.org/10.1007/978-1-4842-8590-9_20

Available Reports

Using the Workplace Analytics homepage or using the Microsoft Teams App you get an overview of the reports that are available for you. From the Workplace Analytics page, you can also download a PowerPoint that provides the same insights as the web interface.

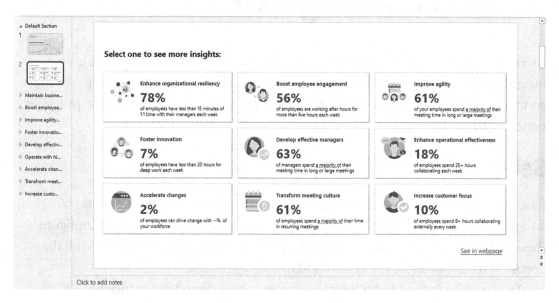

Figure 20-1. *Leader insights in PowerPoint*

Each section of the PowerPoint or section of the Workplace Analytics provides a separate set of reports and insights.

Organizational Resilience

The organizational resilience dashboard provides insights into the work-life balance of employees in the organization. Using metrics driven by work, for example, work done outside of normal business hours and having 1:1 meeting with managers, and team cohesion. From the dashboard several recommendations and best practices are provided to add value to the insights.

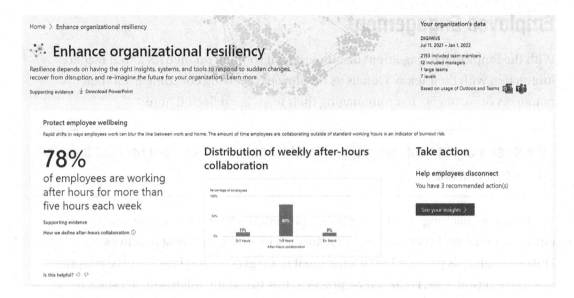

Figure 20-2. *Enhance organizational resilience in Workplace Analytics*

The same data is reflected in the My Organization tab in Microsoft Teams.

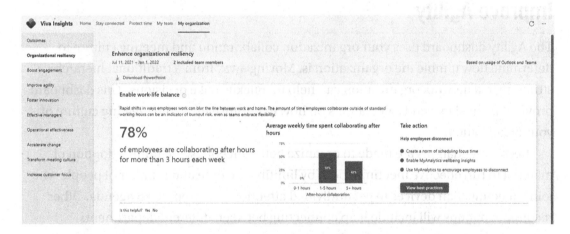

Figure 20-3. *Enhance organizational resilience in the Viva Insights App in Microsoft Teams*

Best practices are grouped in the work-life balance, providing support, helping employees make decisions and focus on cohesion within a team. Each best practice links to either documentation or studies done by Microsoft to provide background information and tips.

Employee Engagement

With the Employee engagement dashboard, you zoom in on metrics about leader interaction with their team. Details as employees receiving coaching from their managers or managers micromanaging their team are reflected here.

For these insights to be available, at least 25 percent of your teams must have five or more members.

Promote coaching and development, prevent burnout, drive employee empowerment, and cohesion within teams are used to group best practices. Documentation is provided as to what great managers do and how to drive adoption of such best practices. Followed by practical tips to use the Microsoft 365 stack to collaborate to drive employee empowerment and insights to recognize employee capacity.

Improve Agility

The Agility dashboard uses your organization collaboration and meeting culture to determine how nimble the organization is. Moving away from a traditional hierarchical structure to a network organization can help to quickly make decisions. This dashboard provides the insights and calculations on how to improve upon the meeting culture of your organization.

Recommendations are made to organize better meetings, including adoption of material to run effective meetings, both by limiting the time and number of people who join a meeting. Ban devices to get undivided attention and prepare an agenda. Other recommendations will include help connecting between different departments

Foster Innovation

Innovation is all about the ability to focus, and this dashboard provides insights into uninterrupted time for work. Without time to focus, employees can feel limited in creativity and innovation.

Recommendations are designed around increasing focus time. Establishing a meeting-free day each week is the first recommendation, including a detailed step-by-step plan to implement such a meeting-free day once a week. Other recommendations highlighted are the implementation of a focus plan and best practices to not disturb colleagues who have a "Focus" status in Microsoft Teams.

Effective Manager

The My organization page provides detailed reports for a manager for personal use. The Effective manager dashboard provides a high-level overview of similar metrics focusing on the manager meetings, having a clear structured decision-making format and the length of meetings.

Recommendations are made to implement all settings of productivity tools as Microsoft Teams to record meetings and keep meeting notes in OneNote for easy access. As with employee engagement, the importance of coaching and regular 1:1 meeting is highlighted as well. Research is provided as to what great managers do on a daily basis to make sure these insights can be adopted by the whole organization.

Operation Effectiveness

Having insights into how employees collaborate within the organization may prove helpful to build a culture that improves the daily work. The dashboard provides an overview of how much time employees spend on collaboration.

With best practices and research, details are provided to kill recurring meetings no longer needed. In-line suggestions in Outlook to be mindful of other people's time and tips to run effective meetings will help to keep meetings to a minimum.

Accelerate Change

Accelerated change focusses on the influencers available within your organization. An overview of the reach of these influencers and their proportion of the organization can help identify how you can communicate change with influencers.

People who have strong networks within the organization can be used to drive adoption of new technology or policies. With this dashboard, you are provided with research on how influencers can help you drive adoption as well as links to use the Microsoft Teams tooling available to share and collaborate to build strong networks.

Transform Meeting Culture

While meetings are an important part of daily business, too many of them can stifle collaboration and productivity. The Transform meeting culture dashboard shows you how employees' and managers' meetings are spent.

Best practices are crafted around optimizing meeting hours, implementing healthy meeting habits such as joining meetings on time and paying attention during the meeting without multitasking.

Increase Customer Focus

External collaboration is often a great indicator for customer focus. The Increase customer focus dashboard uses metrics to track external collaboration. By linking to research and best practices as a leader, you can use these metrics to implement collaboration practices involving the customer. By doing so, you can build long-term relations with your customers and anticipate and engage in a meaningful way.

Conclusion

Using Leader insights, you can get a unique view into the working habits of your organization. Insights that can give you a competitive edge or improve well-being of employees to build a great place to work!

CHAPTER 21

Advanced Insights

After Personal insights, Team insights, and Leader insights, the final part focusses on some of the advanced scenarios available with Viva Insights. These advanced insights require an analyst's mindset. They require an additional role and experience with data analysis tools as Power BI or Python or R.

Setup

These advanced settings require the configuration of Analysts settings and if you are using advanced insights that combines HRM data with Viva Insights you are required to upload that organizational data. Navigate to `https://workplaceanalytics.office.com/` and select Analyst settings to get started. To configure these settings, you need to be assigned the **Insights Administrator** license, the process will take you through four steps:

- Setting up permissions
- Setting up system defaults
- Uploading organizational data
- Data mapping

Using the first step, you are presented the overview of prerequisites like permissions. You need to confirm these settings and make sure that you have handed out permissions.

If you do not want to run these scenarios directly in production, you can build a test setup too, but at least five users with active mailboxes and collaboration behavior are required. These user accounts must all have the same manager.

© D'arce Hess, Albert-Jan Schot, Tracy van der Schyff 2023
D. Hess et al., *Getting Started with Microsoft Viva*, https://doi.org/10.1007/978-1-4842-8590-9_21

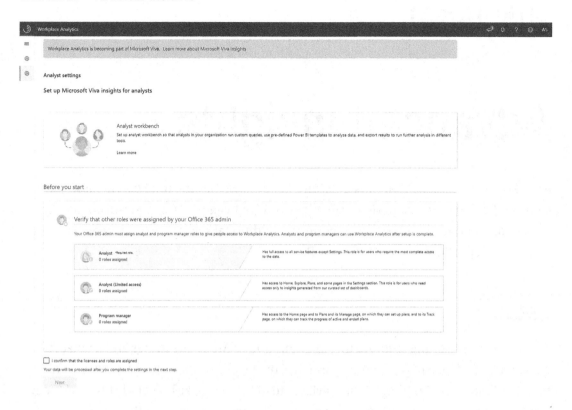

Figure 21-1. *Workplace analytics setting up Analysts settings*

Configuring permissions is done through the Azure Active Directory. Navigate to the Azure Active Directory Admin center. Navigate to the Enterprise Applications, filter on All Applications and search for Workplace Analytics.

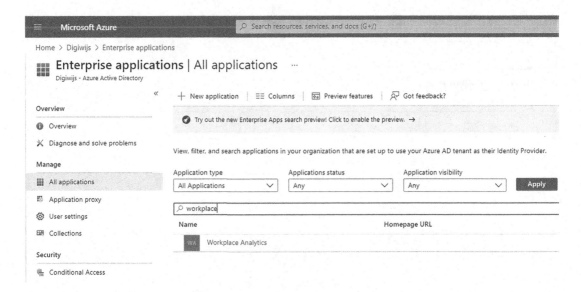

Figure 21-2. *Azure Active Workplace analytics app registration*

From the App registration page, you can assign permissions to users and groups. Select any user or (dynamic) group you want to assign permissions, but keep in mind that they will need the Viva Insights license to be able to access the different settings. You can specify the following permissions:

- **Administrator:** has full access to all settings and can be interchanged with the **Viva Insights Administrator** role

- **Business leader:** has access to the Organizational Insights

- **People manager:** can view My Team insights in Teams and the Viva Insights Home

- **Analyst:** can access all services except data upload and configuration settings

- **Analyst (Limited Access):** has access to reports and insights but not the Query Designer

- **Program manager:** has access to the organizational data and can track Plans

With permissions and licenses in place, the next step is to configure your system default settings specifying the work week and hours and the hourly rate.

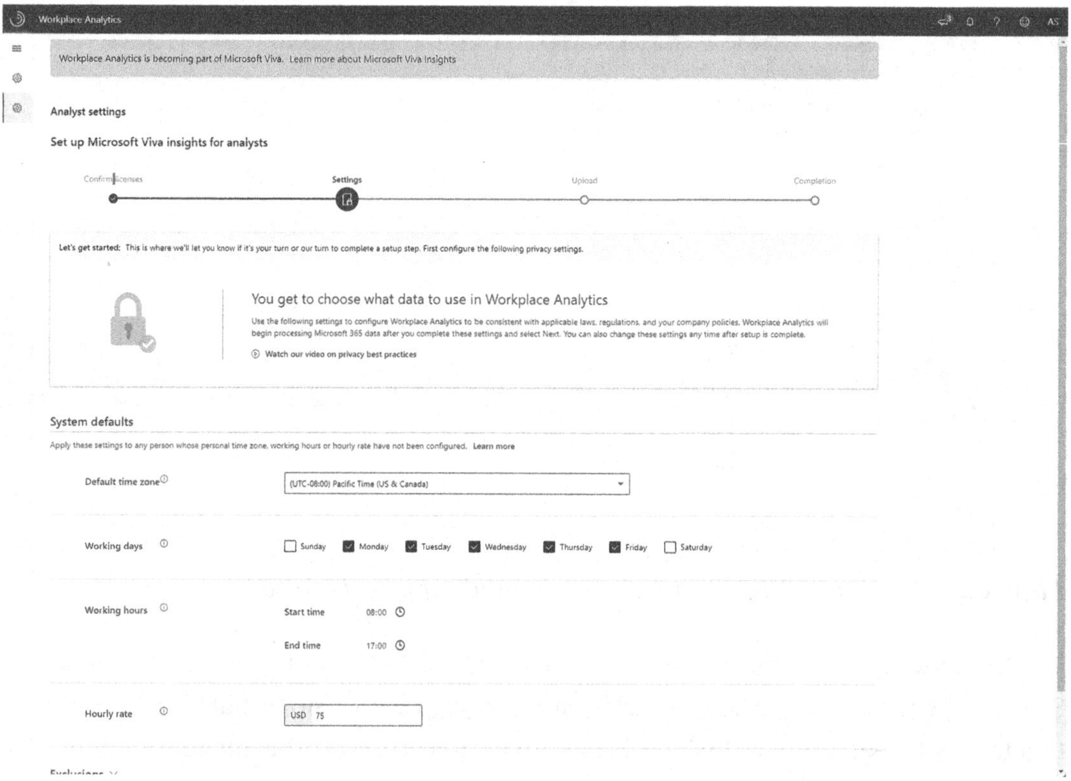

Figure 21-3. *Workplace Analytics System settings*

After the initial configuration, you can update these values, but it will take up to the next refresh (during the next weekend) for changes to show up.

The third step is to upload organizational data. You can download a CSV template and use that to provide the data used in analyzing.

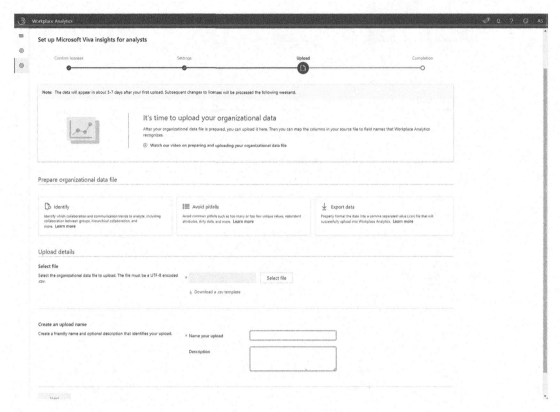

Figure 21-4. *Workplace Analytics upload organizational data*

The template provides a set of required fields, a few optional or reserved fields and the option to add any optional field that you want to use in your analysis.

Figure 21-5. *Organizational data template*

With the Excel prepared, save it as a CSV and upload it. Once uploaded, the data will pass a first validation with basic rules as to validity of the CSV and data input. If the data can be interpreted by the system, you have the option to map fields. Mapping of optional attributes allows you to disable them in the report.

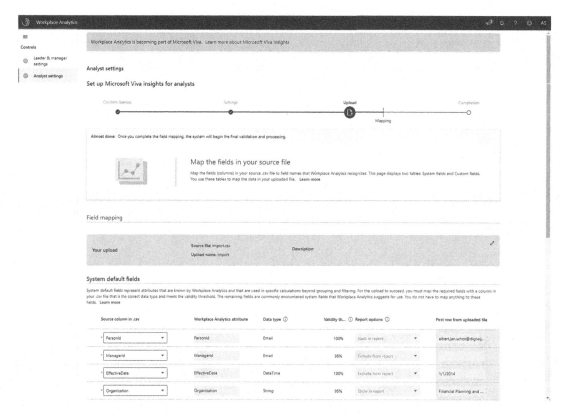

Figure 21-6. *Workplace Analytics map organizational data*

For optional and custom fields, you can choose both the data type and report options. These fields can be used to map unique identifiers to link data together or to add additional data to your reports.

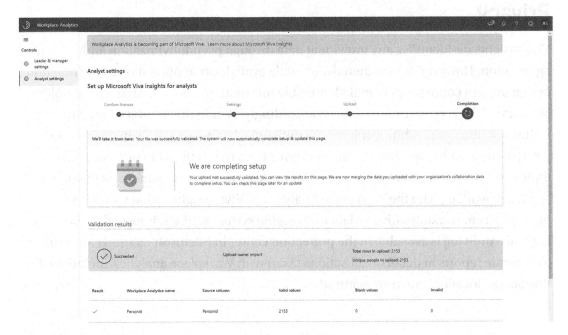

HireDate	▼	HireDate	DateTime		95%	Show in report	▼	1/1/2014

Email
Timezone
Boolean
DateTime
Double
Integer
String

Custom fields (optional)

Custom fields are optional attributes you can create. Select a column from the source .csv file. Name ... lect the data type, set the validity threshold, and select the report option. Learn more

	Source column in .csv		Workplace Analytics attribute			Validity th... ⓘ	Report options ⓘ		First row from uploaded file
🗑	Talent	▼	Talent		String	0 %	Show in report	▼	Technology
🗑	SalesQuota	▼	SalesQuota		Double	0 %	Show in report	▼	100

⊕ Add custom field

☐ I confirm that these mappings are correct.

Submitting this file starts the upload process. If the file passes validation, it will be loaded into the system.

Back   Next

Figure 21-7. *Workplace analytics map custom fields*

With all fields mapped, you can select to import the data. Importing the data can take up to a few hours, depending on the complexity and size of the data set.

Workplace Analytics

Workplace Analytics is becoming part of Microsoft Viva. Learn more about Microsoft Viva Insights

Controls

Leader & manager settings

Analyst settings

Analyst settings

Set up Microsoft Viva insights for analysts

Confirm licenses   Settings   Upload   Completion

We'll take it from here: Your file was successfully validated. The system will now automatically complete setup & update this page.

We are completing setup

Your upload was successfully validated. You can view the results on this page. We are now merging the data you uploaded with your organization's collaboration data to complete setup. You can check this page later for an update

Validation results

Succeeded	Upload name: Import	Total rows in upload: 2153
		Unique people in upload: 2153

Result	Workplace Analytics name	Source column	Valid values	Blank values	Invalid
✓	PersonId	PersonId	2153	0	0

Figure 21-8. *Workplace analytics completed data import*

If the data is successfully validated and processed, you can expect to use the insights once the setup is completed. If the data validation fails, you can download the error log to see additional details and can choose to change either the CSV or mapping of your fields.

When preparing the CSV for upload, some basic CSV rules apply:

- All column names must be only letters and numbers (alphanumeric characters)

- Must have at least one lowercase letter

- No spaces or non-alphanumeric characters are allowed

- A column must always start with a letter

You can upload new iterations of your dataset once the data is processed to make sure everything stays up to date.

Privacy

Viva Insights de-identifies any individual data through pseudonymization and aggregation. However, data gathered and made available in reports such as the function or department counts as personal identifiable information. As an analyst, you should be aware of these ramifications and act accordingly. Within the Analyst Configuration settings, an analyst or administrator can configure what data is visible in queries and dashboards, exclude specific domains or terms from the result set to prevent sensitive topics from showing up or hash subject lines to keep data as anonymous as possible.

When working with the Workplace Analytics or Viva Insights, what you do as a manager, from working with the data to changing system settings, is logged in the Audit log. This Audit log is available in the protection center in Microsoft 365 and can be used to generate reports in detail on all actions taken with Workplace analytics, including the timestamp, location, and browser used.

Figure 21-9. *Workplace analytics Audit log*

Plans

Workplace Analytics provides the option to create plans that drive improvement of a specific metric. Plans allow you to gather a group of people and focus on a single metric to improve. Currently, there are several sample plans available to improve the number of focus hours or reducing meeting load.

Plans can be set up and configured by Analysts, Limited Analysts, and Program managers. Running for a specific period, participants of a plan will be presented both in-line suggestions in Outlook and sections in their briefing e-mails.

- **Focus** is used to highlight the importance of focus and boost an increase in focus time among participants.

- **Collaboration** is used to decrease the number of meeting hours.

- **Well-being** focusses on decreasing the number of collaboration hours and meetings run outside of the participants working hours.

- **Seller success** prioritizes network building for participants.

Setting up a new plan allows you to select the duration and target participants either using a CSV file to upload the participants by name or using the Viva Insights available metrics.

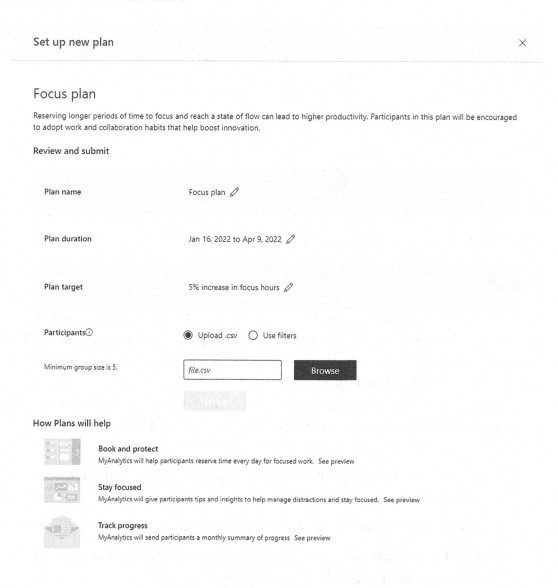

Figure 21-10. *Starting a new focus plan*

Once a plan is created, you can track to monitor progress of the plan and use that input to support your goal with additional adoption materials.

Analyze Data

To work with the Viva Insights or Workplace Analytics data as an analyst, you need to be assigned the Analyst or Analyst (limited) role. Without this role, even as an administrator, you will not be able to view or edit the queries.

Query Designer

The query designer allows you to write custom queries to leverage the data available in Workplace analytics. You can use existing templates or write custom queries yourself. Navigating to the query designer as an analyst provides you with the option to create a new query or use one of the featured templates.

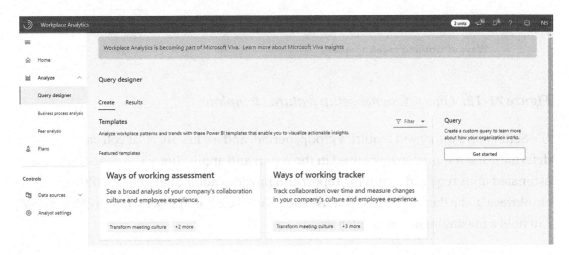

Figure 21-11. *Query designer overview*

Using a featured template walks you through the different queries and settings to set up. It will point to both Power BI documentation and the configuration of the required queries. Queries will gather the information required to gather insights.

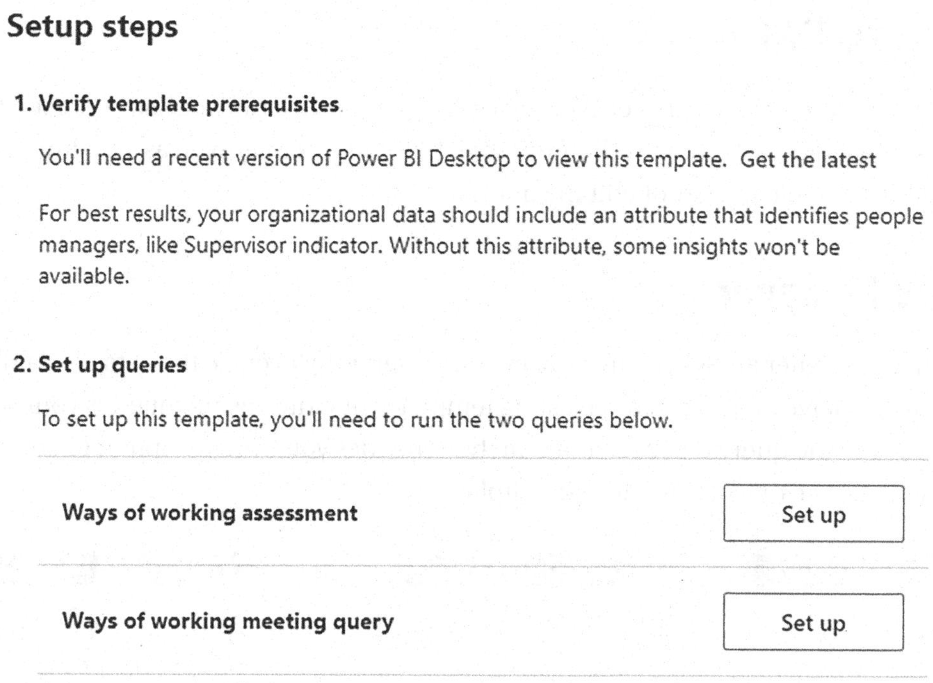

Setup steps

1. Verify template prerequisites

You'll need a recent version of Power BI Desktop to view this template. Get the latest

For best results, your organizational data should include an attribute that identifies people managers, like Supervisor indicator. Without this attribute, some insights won't be available.

2. Set up queries

To set up this template, you'll need to run the two queries below.

Ways of working assessment	Set up
Ways of working meeting query	Set up

Figure 21-12. *Query designer setup featured template*

Setting up a query will require a group, period, and exclusion. Next you can determine the required metrics used in the report and apply filters. The page shows the estimated units required to run the report and provides additional filters to filter out employees of the data set. When you use the CSV to select employees, beware that a CSV can hold a maximum of 150 employees.

Ways of working assessment

Analyze collaboration and engagement in Power BI. Requires Standard meetin...

Group by	Time period			Exclusions
Week ▼	Last 6 months ▼	☐ Auto-refresh ⓘ Sun. 07/04/2021 to Sat. 01/01/2022		(1) Selected exclusions ▼

❶ Select metrics

What do you want to know about these employees? ⓘ

*   Select ... ▼

Base Metric	Type	Display Name				
Emails sent	Count	Emails sent to 50 or more recipients	✎	⬚	🗑	↑↓
Emails sent	Count	Emails sent 11 to 50 recipients	✎	⬚	🗑	↑↓
Emails sent	Count	Emails sent 6 to 10 recipients	✎	⬚	🗑	↑↓
Emails sent	Count	Emails sent 2 to 5 recipients	✎	⬚	🗑	↑↓
Emails sent	Count	Emails sent 1 recipient	✎	⬚	🗑	↑↓

Figure 21-13. *Query configuration*

Exclusions allows for filtering out data before running the report. By default, there is an exclusion rule that filters out specific types of meetings. By filtering out cancelled meetings, you can be sure that the results of those meetings are not showing up in metrics around productivity or working outside of working hours.

Analyst settings > Meeting exclusion > **View meeting exclusion**

Tenant Default Meeting Exclusion Rule

Summary of meetings that remain	Attendee meeting hours	Number of meetings
After each exclusion is applied, this summary updates to reflect what remains in your analysis	47% 430 of 918 total	65% 316 of 486 total

Summary of the exclusion rule

🔒
Exclusions are not editable.

	Attendee meeting hours	Number of meetings
Exclude cancelled meetings exclude all meetings that are cancelled 0 keywords excluded	0% 0 out of 918 total meeting hours	0% 0 out of 486 total meetings

Figure 21-14. *Exclusion rule*

239

Once finished, you can run your query and await the results to be processed. These results can then be used in Power BI, Excel, or any other data analysis tool.

Consumption Model

With Microsoft Viva Insights Capacity, you get additional consumption units added to your environment. Running queries use these units based on their consumption. When designing a query, you get an estimate of the number of units it will take to execute the query and work with the results.

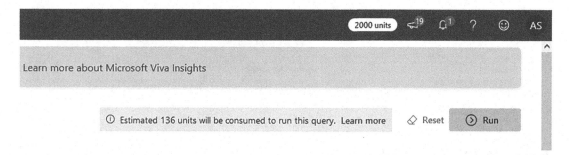

Figure 21-15.   *Consumption model*

Peer Analysis

Another advanced scenario supported for analysts is the availability of peer analysis. With this option, you can compare two groups of people within the organization. These insights can be used to identify unique work habits and highlight those so that the whole company can benefit from them.

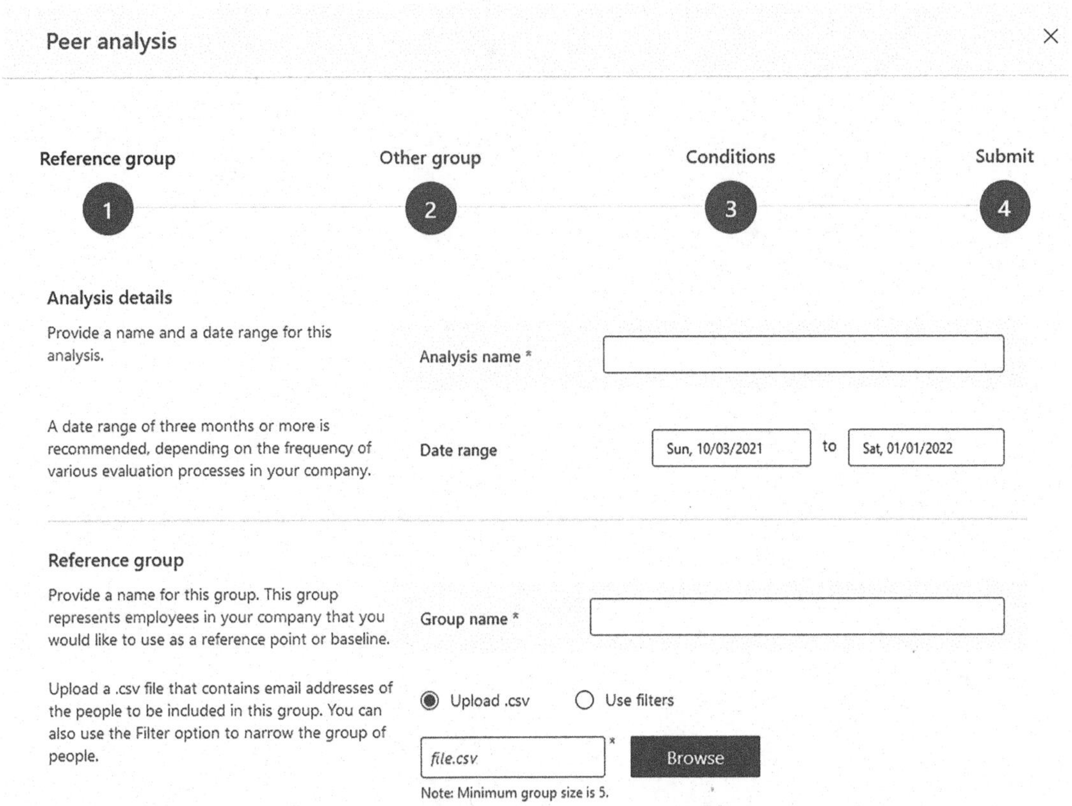

Figure 21-16. *Peer analysis*

The peer analysis then uses the different metrics captured by Viva Insights to provide highlights. You can compare 1:1 meeting hours or collaboration outside of business hours as metrics to compare these groups and find valuable insights.

Conclusion

Advanced insights can provide a lot of additional value on top of the personal and manager insights Viva Insights already provides your organization with. Yet working with the advanced insights requires some experience with data science. The documentation does provide ample samples and explanation as to why certain trends are showing; but there is a risk to mix up cause and effect when working with this type of data.

APPENDIX

Hyperlink Resources for the Book

Hyperlinks added as resources for the book

Chapter 3 Microsoft Viva Introduction

Microsoft Viva Licensing

Microsoft Viva Service Descriptions

https://docs.microsoft.com/en-us/office365/servicedescriptions/microsoft-viva-service-description

Chapter 4 Microsoft Viva Learning

What is adoption?

In the *Accelerating Modern Workplace Productivity Adoption* e-book,

https://adoption.microsoft.com/wp-content/uploads/2020/06/Accelerating-Modern-Workplace-Productivity-Adoption.pdf

Chapter 4 Microsoft Viva Learning

What is adoption?

"Microsoft 365 Adoption Hub"

https://adoption.microsoft.com/

Chapter 4 Microsoft Viva Learning

The impact of training on adoption

"The Total Economic Impact™ Of Microsoft Teams"

https://techcommunity.microsoft.com/t5/microsoft-teams-blog/quantifying-the-value-of-collaboration-with-microsoft-teams/ba-p/481328#:~:text=Forrester%20study%3A%20The%20Total%20Economic%20Impact%E2%84%A2%20Of%20Microsoft,study%3A%20The%20Total%20Economic%20Impact%E2%84%A2%20Of%20Microsoft%20Teams.

© D'arce Hess, Albert-Jan Schot, Tracy van der Schyff 2023
D. Hess et al., *Getting Started with Microsoft Viva*, https://doi.org/10.1007/978-1-4842-8590-9

Chapter 4 Microsoft Viva Learning

Microsoft Teams Analytics and Reporting

Teams admin center

Microsoft Teams admin center

`https://admin.teams.microsoft.com/`

Chapter 4 Microsoft Viva Learning

Microsoft Productivity Score

`https://docs.microsoft.com/en-US/microsoft-365/admin/productivity/productivity-score?WT.mc_id=365AdminCSH_inproduct&view=o365-worldwide`

Chapter 5 Microsoft Viva Learning

Product overview

With the launch of Microsoft Viva, Microsoft published an e-book, *The People-Powered Workplace.*

`https://info.microsoft.com/CA-TeamPlat-WBNR-FY21-05May-03-ThePeopleP oweredWorkplaceReimaginetheEmployeeExperience-SRGCM4626_01Registration-ForminBody.html`

Chapter 8 Microsoft Viva Connections

Intranet Groundwork

SharePoint Look Book

`https://lookbook.microsoft.com/`

Chapter 10 Microsoft Viva Connections

Access the Dashboard

Technical Resources

`https://learn.microsoft.com/en-us/viva/connections/create-dashboard`

Set up global navigation in the SharePoint app bar | Microsoft Docs

`https://docs.microsoft.com/en-us/viva/connections/sharepoint-app-bar`

Chapter 10 Microsoft Viva Connections

Configure the Viva Connections App in the Admin Center

Manage Apps

`https://admin.teams.microsoft.com/policies/manage-apps`

Index

A

Accelerated change, 225
Administrator
    records management, 139
    roles/responsibilities, 140, 141
    settings control, 139
Adoption
    vs. consumption, 16
    definition, 16
    framework, 17
    measurement, 23
    phases, 16, 17
    resources, 16
    training, 17–19
Agility dashboard, 224
AI-suggested topics
    AWS, 146
    checklist, 147
    confirming, 151
    knowledge
        manager, 146, 147
    published topics, 152
    removed topics, 152, 153
    types, 146
Alternate names, 150, 154
Amazon Web Services (AWS), 146
Artificial intelligence (AI), 104
Audit log, 234, 235
Azure Active Directory, 125, 174, 182, 213,
        218, 228

B

Book focus time, 174, 183, 210
Briefing e-mail, 177
    book focus time, 210
    excerpt, 209
    follow up on tasks, 210
    headspace meditation, 210
    Outlook client, 208
    plan your week, 210
    prepare for meetings, 210
Business partners/associated skills, 140
Business scenarios, 103, 104

C

Change management, 16, 17, 33,
        69, 85, 100
Change Management Journey, 15
Consumption model, 15, 240
CSV, 230, 231, 234, 235, 238

D

Dashboards, Viva insights home, 183
    cards, 203
    collaboration, 206–208
    focus
        plan results, 204
        plan setup, 203, 204
        time, 204

© D'arce Hess, Albert-Jan Schot, Tracy van der Schyff 2023
D. Hess et al., *Getting Started with Microsoft Viva*, https://doi.org/10.1007/978-1-4842-8590-9

Dashboards, Viva insights home (*cont.*)
    network, 205, 206
    quiet days overview, 205
    well-being, 204, 205
Default off, 181
Default on, 181
Delay Delivery Plan, 180, 202, 205
Digest e-mail, 174, 180, 208, 211, 219

E, F

Effective manager dashboard, 225
eLearning, 20
e-mails, 174
Employee engagement, 4, 76, 81, 167, 174,
    224, 225
Employee experience platform (EXP), 4,
    6, 11, 74
Employees
    environment, 18
    time, 18
    training, 18
    video training, 22
Exchange Online, 173, 179, 182, 185
Exchange Online mailbox, 172, 187, 215
Explicit knowledge, 134–137

G

General Data Protection Regulation
    (GDPR), 173
Get-MyAnalyticsFeatureConfig, 182
Group insights, 213, 218, 221
Group-to-group metrics, 176

H

Hands-on training, 21
Headspace, 194
Headspace meditation, 210

I, J

Implicit knowledge, 134, 135, 137
Impressions, 149
Innovation, 224
Insights Administrator, 182, 213, 221
Insights Business Leader, 182, 221
Instructor-led training, 20
Intranets
    Intelligent Intranet, 74
    purpose, 73
    workplace, 74
IT/business disparity, 15
IT support process, 18

K

Knowledge Management
    definition, 133
    Viva Topics, 133
Knowledge manager
    contribution areas, 141
    definition, 141
    required permissions, 142
    skills and responsibilities, 142
Knowledge types
    explicit, 134
    implicit, 134, 135
    tacit, 135

L

Language support, 165
Leader insights, 175, 180, 181, 226
  accelerated change, 225
  Agility dashboard, 224
  effective manager, 225
  employee engagement, 224
  foster innovation, 224, 225
  increase customer focus
      dashboard, 226
  operation effectiveness, 225
  organizational resilience, 222, 223
  PowerPoint, 222
  privacy, 221
  setup, 221
  transform meeting culture, 226
  Workplace Analytics homepage, 222
Learning cultures, 22, 23
Learning management system, 34, 54, 55
LinkedIn learning courses
  business courses, 38, 39
  creative courses, 39
  skills courses, 40
  tech courses, 40

M

Manager insights, 174, 180, 219
  briefing e-mails, 218
  digest e-mails, 218, 219
  group insights, 213, 218
  leader/manager settings, 214
  privacy, 215
  setup, 213–215
  team insights, 215–217
Manually curated topics
  creating new topic, 153–155
  definition, 153

expected time frames, 156
  removing new topic, 155
Meeting metrics, 176
Microsoft
  analytics, 23, 24
  measurement, 23, 24
Microsoft productivity score, 27
  communication, 29
  content collaboration, 31
  documentation, 27
  main dashboard, 28
  meetings, 30
  report, 27
  supplied areas, 28
  team work, 32
Microsoft's corporate mission, 22
Microsoft's leadership principles, 23
Microsoft Teams Analytics and
      Reporting, 26, 27
Microsoft Teams, 78, 162, 163, 170
  headspace, 194
  protect time, 196
  reflections, 190, 191
  Send Praise, 191–193
  settings, 196, 197
  stay connected
      meeting reminders, 195
      meeting suggestions, 195
      mentions, 196
      outstanding tasks, 195
      unread documents share, 196
      upcoming meeting, 196
  virtual commute, 193, 194
  Viva Personal Insights features, 189
Microsoft Teams App, 222
Microsoft 365 plans, 173, 179
Microsoft 365 usage analytics, 26
Microsoft 365 usage report, 24, 25

Microsoft Viva
   Ally.io, 11
   definition, 4
   elements, 3, 4
   EXP, 6
   modules, 6, 34
   Viva Connections, 6, 7
   Viva Insights, 6, 8
   Viva Learning, 6, 7
   Viva Topics, 6, 8
Microsoft Viva Insights, 180
   aspects, 169
   dashboard for end users, 170
   dashboard for leaders, 172
   dashboard for managers, 171
   privacy, 172, 173
Microsoft Viva modules
   advanced analysis, 173
   analysis capabilities, 175
   integration, 175
   leader insights, 175
   manager insights, 174
   personal Insights, 173, 174
Microsoft Viva Personal Insights, 173, 174
Microsoft Viva Topics, 101, 116, 125, 135
My Organization dashboard, 171
My Team insights, 181

N

Network, 205, 206
Network metrics, 176

O

Organizational resilience, 222, 223
Outlook add-in, 180, 185
   time away
      focus time, 199
      inline suggestions, 202
      meeting suggestions, 201
      outstanding tasks, 201
      public holidays, 198
      schedule, 199
      set lunch hours, 201
      track e-mail and document open
        rates, 201, 202
      unread documents, 201
      upcoming meetings, 200
   Viva insights, 197, 198
Outlook Add-in, 172, 174

P

Peer analysis, 240, 241
Peer comparison metrics, 176
Personal insights
   actions, 183
   dashboards (*see* Dashboards, Viva
      insights home)
   email reminders
      briefing e-mail, 208–210
      digests, 211
   exchange online setup, 185
   Microsoft Teams, 183, 188
   Microsoft teams setup, 184, 185
   MyAnalytics, 183
   Outlook (*see* Outlook add-in)
   privacy, 187, 188
   teams/outlook, 183
   triggers, 183
Person metrics, 176
Person-to-person
      metrics, 176
Pomodoro technique, 35

PowerShell, 83, 84, 107, 182
Praise functionality, 177, 191, 193
Privacy, 187, 188, 215, 221
PrivacyMode parameter, 182
Published Topics, 152

Q

Quality Score, 148
Query configuration, 239
Query designer, 238
    configuration, 239
    exclusion rule, 239
    featured template, 237, 238
    overview, 237
Quiet hours impact
    report, 217

R

Removed Topics, 145, 152, 153
R-script library, 181

S

Set-MyAnalyticsFeatureConfig, 182
Set-UserBriefingConfig, 182
SharePoint
    communication sites, 74
    configuration, 46, 47
    document types, 45
    highlights, 158, 159
    source materials
        preparation, 47, 48
        reference, 49, 50
Simulation training, 20
Staff Reductions, 147
Suggested people, 149, 150

T

Tacit knowledge, 135, 137
Team insights, 216
    Quiet hours impact report, 217
    team meeting habits, 217
    Viva Insights Home, 215
Team meeting habits, 217
Teams Admin center app policies, 184
3rd party content providers, 55, 56
Topic Cards, 137
Topic Center, 141, 165
Topic Center, AI-suggested topics
    alternate names, 150
    discovered, 149
    impressions, 149
    knowledge managers, 148
    name, 149
    quality score, 148
    site collections, 148
    suggested people, 149, 150
Topic contributors
    description, 142
    required permissions, 143
    skills and responsibilities, 143
Topic locations
    Microsoft Teams, 162, 163
    office application search, 160
    search results, 159
    SharePoint highlights, 158, 159
    Topic Center, 165
    Yammer posts, 160–162
Track e-mail and document open rates,
    201, 202
Training programs
    learning methods, 20, 21
    learning styles, 19, 20
    styles/methods, 21, 22

U

Ultradian Rhythm, 35
Understanding security
    guests and external users, 157
    source content, 145
    SharePoint sites, 157
    user requirements, 156

V

Virtual commute, 177, 193, 194
Viva connections, 75, 76
    Admin Center, 97, 98
    change Management, 100
    concepts/capabilities, 77
    content, 97
    curated *vs.* tailored
        experience, 80
    dashboard
        access, 95, 96
        adding cards, 92
        audience, 94, 95
        configuration, cards, 93
        creation, 91
        layout, 93, 94
    desktop experience, 79
    Finding Stuff, 84–86
    global way finding, 86, 87
    home site, 83
        PowerShell, 84
        SharePoint Admin Center, 83, 84
    instructions, 81, 82
    Intranet, 82, 83, 100
    languages, 80
    Microsoft 365 apps integration, 76
    mobile experience, 78
    policies, 98–100
    SharePoint app bar, 87

content, 87, 88
    Global Navigation, 88–90
Viva Dashboard, 180
Viva insights
    meeting suggestion, 195
    opt-out, 188
    Outlook (*see* Outlook add-in)
    pop out, 194
    praise reminder notification, 193
    reflections history, 190
    reflections settings, 191
    send praise, 192
    send praise as a message, 192
    teams, 186
    teams app settings, 197
    teams overview, 189
Viva Insights add-on, 181
Viva Insights add-on license, 180
Viva Insights Capacity, 175, 181
Viva Insights licenses, 179
Viva Learning
    access, 50, 51
    autonomy, 35
    benefits, 35
    customizable experience, 33
    definition, 33
    empowering, 69
    featured sets, 52–54
    Home tab, 59
        add interests, 61, 62
        Browse Courses, 60
        engaging, courses, 61
        filters, 60
    licensing
        features, 37, 38
        free version, 37
        LinkedIn Enterprise courses, 38–40
    Manage tab

add courses, 68, 69

add Tab, channel, 68

recommendation details, 67

remove courses, 69

Microsoft Teams, 34, 57

My Learning tab

embed learning, chat
conversations, 65–67

navigation, 62, 63

recommended courses, 64

sharing courses, 65

update status, 63, 64

navigation

pin, 57, 58

Show me around, 58, 59

pillars, 35, 36

purpose, 34

recommend content, 51, 52

roles, 41

setting

blocking, 43, 44

employees, pin, 42, 43

SharePoint, 45, 47–50

sources, 44, 45

tasks, 35

3rd party content providers, 55, 56

training, 34

Viva metrics, 175, 176

Viva Topics

Admin Center

active sites, 122, 124

set-up process, 117–120

AI, 104, 126

applications, 137

common search problems, 136

companies, 104

excluding, 122–124

knowledge management

free trial, 111

licensing requirements, 110

SharePoint, 105

Teams, 105–107

Yammer, 107–109

members, 104

options, 125

permissions

Admin Center, 127

creation/editing, 127, 128

managing, 128

sites, 120–122

source of truth, 137

technical planning

Add-On, 114, 115

layers, 113

licenses, 116, 117

making decisions, 113

Viva Suite, 115

Topic Center

Admin Center, 129

confirmation page, 130, 131

creation, 130

managing, 131, 132

naming, 129

setting, 129

Topic Visibility, 126

W, X

Well-being dashboard, 176, 204, 205

Workplace analytics, 180

analyze data

consumption model, 240

peer analysis, 240, 241

query designer, 237–240

Workplace analytics (*cont.*)
    Audit log, 235
    Azure Active workplace analytics app
        registration, 229
    completed data import, 233
    map custom fields, 233
    map organizational data, 232
    organizational data
        template, 231
    plans, 235, 236

    privacy, 234
    setting up analysts settings, 228
    setup, 227–234
    system settings, 230
    upload organizational data, 231

Y, Z

Yammer, 9, 78, 80, 97, 100, 107, 108, 111,
        137, 158, 160–162

Printed in the United States
by Baker & Taylor Publisher Services

Printed in the United States
by Baker & Taylor Publisher Services